The Untethered Relationship

The Untethered Relationship

Experience Your Unimaginable Capacity for Love

Chris G. Moon

GREENLEAF
BOOK GROUP PRESS

Published by Greenleaf Book Group Press
Austin, Texas
www.gbgpress.com

Distributed by Greenleaf Book Group

For ordering information or special discounts for bulk purchases, please contact Greenleaf Book Group at PO Box 91869, Austin, TX 78709, 512.891.6100.

Design and composition by Jan Westendorp, Kato Design and Photo
Cover design by Greenleaf Book Group and Jan Westendorp
Figures 8.2–8.6 on pages 227–231 by Jan Westendorp.
All photos should include a credit line adjacent to the photo.
Cover image Copyright thanom. Used under license from Shutterstock.com

Cataloging-in-Publication data is available.

Print ISBN: 978-1-62634-390-0

eBook ISBN: 978-1-62634-391-7

Part of the Tree Neutral® program, which offsets the number of trees consumed in the production and printing of this book by taking proactive steps, such as planting trees in direct proportion to the number of trees used: www.treeneutral.com

Printed in the United States of America on acid-free paper

17 18 19 20 21 22   10 9 8 7 6 5 4 3 2 1

First Edition

Dedication

To *You*

Acknowledgments

I have great appreciation for the many teachers and friends whom I have encountered at various stages of my life.

Su Mei, Harmon, and Tara: my greatest relationship teachers, you have enriched my life beyond description!

Tiffany Chang: a truly generous, openhearted soul. Thank you for being my friend and for supporting me for so many years.

Jyoti and Priti: for supporting and promoting my work in China, and for being such beautiful angels for me, Su Mei, Tara, and Harmon.

David Schnarch: his insights on the purpose of irritation in relationships, and the difference between love and need for importance opened my eyes to the purpose of relationship.

Robert Scheinfeld: for his clarity in explaining the dynamics of awakening, and for his insights on appreciation as a key to *process* and beyond.

Jed McKenna: Jed introduced "emotional adulthood" to me and in general rocked my world with his book *Spiritual Enlightenment: The Damnedest Thing*.

Jane Nelsen: her book *Positive Discipline* opened my eyes to how our needs for belonging and significance influence all our pursuits, as well as our relationship behaviors.

Chuck Spezzano: Chuck introduced me to his version of the "Polarities Model," and I adapted it somewhat. It is one of only three models that I continued working with after popping out of the trance state.

Gay and Kathlyn Hendricks: for the Loop of Awareness.

Peter Dziuban: I heartily recommend *Simply Notice*, one of the most beautifully simple books about who *You* are.

Victor Chen: Victor showed me a simple three-circle model he was playing with and it planted the seed for my "Circles of Expression" model.

Stephen Karpman: his Drama Triangle was the inspiration and foundation for my "Story Prison."

My promoters, past and present: Soo Yew, Yvonne, Joy Wind and Robert, Janice, Rene, Kelly, Tracey, Jeanette, Michael Myers, Marsha and Don, Guy and Rachel, Tai Fu and Mei Chih, Toshitaka and Chieko, Yuko and Masataka, Dena, Peter and Sherri, Carolyn, Doug, Andre, Marie, Vivian, Maya, Kiss, Sita, Yi Ming, the dedicated members of Life-Coach Alliance in China.

My amazingly gifted longtime translators: Udaya, Kwee In, Abbey, Ling, Yuko, Maki, and Louise, whose creative genius and talent built bridges so that I could connect with the hearts of the people I have been fortunate to meet in the past thirty years.

The participants and staff of my workshops and trainings: Because my character as a student tends to be hesitant and stubborn, I guess I needed a few thousand teachers to get through to me. You have been a powerful force in my life and have inspired me beyond belief. I am filled with awe, love, and gratitude when I think of you.

Margaret Moon, Paul Galewitz, Rene Febbraro, and Su Mei Moon: my initial "editors" who provided the emotional support for me to complete and publish this book. Their honesty and clarity made this work complete.

And lastly, a huge thank-you to Steve Donahue, my literary catalyst and coach.

Contents

Preface

I OFFER THIS BOOK AS A WAY to support you to have a direct experience of the true happiness that *You* actually are. It can also help you to recognize the parts that your spouse, children, parents, siblings, and close friends have played as your key supporters in helping you know the truth about yourself. Through this book, I will share how your key relationships support you to have a *direct experience* of—

- Who and what you really are

- Who and what your partner really is

- The purpose of your life

- True, unconditional happiness

- An ever-deepening sense of awe, love, and gratitude

- Harmony and flow in your partnership

- Unconditional love

- Emotional adulthood

A note about "emotional adulthood": I first read this term in a book by Jed McKenna, and it resonated with me more deeply than the better-known terms "emotional maturity" and "emotional intelligence," or "EQ." When I was eleven or twelve years old, I noticed that, although people seemed to grow up physically and mentally, our emotional development did not seem to follow a consistent timeline or keep up with our physical growth. I often witnessed my parents behaving like children when it came to dealing with relationship problems and conflicts. Then, when I got married, I became more aware of my own childish reactions to the discomforts, hurts, and irritations that spousal and parent/child relationships seem so adept at bringing up. I recognized that my angry withdrawals, verbal attacks, and passive aggressiveness were expressed in a slightly more sophisticated manner than when I was four years old, but the emotional reactions were virtually unchanged from that time. A tantrum is a tantrum. When I felt hurt, I got angry and accused others of being responsible for my discomfort. Since I was presenting myself to the public as a relationship counselor and wanted to walk the talk, I applied myself to facing the uncomfortable feelings in my relationships and improving myself as a husband, father, son, brother, and friend.

On top of all the spiritual searching I did before I got married, I spent another eighteen years working on personal growth, spiritual/psychological healing, self-improvement, raising my EQ, conflict resolution, transformative communication, and simple marriage counseling. Eventually, I came to a very discouraging revelation: Growing up was damn hard work! And although I could appreciate that the quality of my life had improved somewhat, I was still far from adulthood, having grown from an emotional six-year-old to an emotional boy of eight. After redefining and reframing my feelings in more than a hundred different ways, I came to the conclusion that I just didn't like feeling vulnerable. Pain was an enemy, and anyone who seemed to make me feel that pain appeared as an adversary before me. Well, if there is one thing that a spouse is really good at, it's making you aware of your vulnerability—your weakness, insecurity, fears, and all aspects of emotional discomfort. Your children can also have that affect, as can your parents, siblings . . . pretty much anyone you form a relationship with.

Then one day I woke up, and I realized that becoming an emotional adult meant understanding what feelings really are. So the next time a discomfort arose, I ignored my usual tendencies to try to fix, heal, transform, or cover the feeling over with positive or spiritual affirmations and simply accepted the feeling as I perceived it to be. That is when I realized what real "process" is.

Process: The word "process" will often appear throughout this book, and it is an important tool in becoming an emotional adult as well as transforming your relationships. When discomfort arises and you respond to it with acceptance instead of rejection, feelings can be perceived as energy patterns registered by kinesthetic sensations in the body. There is really only one pain, but it's interpreted differently by its location, intensity, and duration. Thus you have the experiences of jealousy, sadness, arthritis, or a migraine—all the same pain, but with different stories to support it. Many stories in your intimate relationship can revolve around how your partner seems to have hurt, upset, annoyed, or angered you, bringing up a degree of pain or discomfort. With detached observation, one sees pain as an agitated energy that appears to grow calmer and, as awareness increases, is recognized as the joyful, peaceful energy of one's essence—the marvelously creative, intuitive, loving genius that is one's natural state. Beyond that essence, only the Ineffable (Tao) remains, and there is no separation between the experience and the experiencer. This acceptance of feeling, and direct experience of what lies hidden behind that feeling, is *process* and is what your relationship offers you the opportunity to experience.

The purpose of this book, like the purpose of your important relationships, is to help you to have a direct experience of the magnificent being you truly are. As your awareness of who you are expands in your day-to-day life, you will grow more and more in appreciation of your partner, children, parents, siblings, and all the people in your life, and you will see, on a daily basis, how truly abundant your life is. I hope you enjoy the life-changing journey this book is about to take you on. Bon voyage!

Principles of an Untethered Relationship

This book is written in such a way that you do not have to follow the sequence of the chapters but can choose what most attracts you from each chapter's summary principles, listed below, and take it from there:

1. My partner[1] is not the source of my happiness; I am.

2. My partner is not the cause of my unhappiness or pain.

----

1   Throughout this book, I use the word "partner" mostly to indicate your mate, spouse, or the person with whom you are sharing an intimate relationship. However, if I am describing a situation that for you might describe a relationship to one of your children, parents, siblings, or other acquaintances, you can replace the term "partner" in your mind with the name of that person, and the message will remain true to its purpose.

3. No matter how hard I try, I cannot change my partner.

4. Relationship problems are just stories.

5. Specialness is not love.

6. My partner supports me to grow in acceptance, awareness, and appreciation.

7. My partner and I each have our own boat.

8. Communication with my partner reflects emotional maturity and consciousness.

Bonus Principle

I am the one that I've been looking for.

I'd Be Perfectly Happy, If Only . . .

Principle #1: My partner is not the source of my happiness; I am.

I WAS LEADING A WORKSHOP one day when a woman brought up a problem she was having with her boyfriend. Actually, the problem was that he no longer wanted to be her boyfriend, and she was extremely distraught; overcome by feelings of abandonment, unworthiness, and the heartbreak of crushing disappointment at what she saw as his betrayal. For a short while, she expressed how unwanted and unlovable she felt, giving examples of her faults and shortcomings. Then she went on to express how much she needed him to give her a sense of value. According to her, he was a really great guy—good-looking, strong, financially successful, and possessing a wonderful sense of fun and humor. He was everything she could want in a man.

What I said next, I blurted out before I could get control of my mouth.

"Why would he want to be with you?"

"What do you mean?" she asked, stunned by the brazen challenge.

"I mean, he's this perfect guy, and you've been telling us that you're such a weak, useless, unlovable woman," I said. "Why would he want to be with you?"

Now, I was a young workshop leader at the time and very new to the field of relationship counseling, so I was careless with my overall approach. I was especially careless with the use of the word "why," which people in a vulnerable state often find to be a challenging word that lacks compassion and understanding. However, my question really set off the participant, and after sobbing heavily for a while, she acknowledged that she had put this guy on a pedestal, an attitude that generally tends to leave one down there on the ground, feeling small and insignificant. She admitted her beliefs about herself and how they colored her perception of any prospective partner and then realized it was a script she had acted out over a dozen times in her forty-two years of life.

This story illustrates a common belief that human beings have, one that overshadows almost all intimate relationships in this day and age: "I am incomplete and not good enough and need someone or something from outside to complete me and make me a better person." This is reinforced by other beliefs such as "I must find the one that can complete me," and "I must do something to earn that which will complete me," or "I must prove that I am worthy of the love and happiness I need in order to feel complete," et cetera. All of these statements are the opposite of what is actually true.

In general, human beings seem to take a very long time to realize that no one has the power to make them happy. No matter how often we are disappointed, we continue the attempts at getting the other person to say or do something that will somehow transfer the experience of happiness and fulfillment into our bodies, thus *completing* us. Even countless disappointments in your partner do not necessarily bring about the wisdom and understanding that seem so obvious when they are realized. Instead, after many failed attempts with that so-called one true love, we come to an entirely different conclusion—we conclude that we simply chose the wrong partner! We don't question the belief that someone or something outside of us holds the key to our happiness or what that belief implies about who we are. No, we reinforce the belief by either continuing our outward pursuit, or falling into discouragement and despair. Either way, we remain blind to the truth.

You are the love and happiness that you have been looking for.

In order to more fully experience the above statement, I invite you to confront the beliefs you have held about the purpose and dynamics of relationship and question their validity. Think of it as "leaving the flock." If you consider your beliefs about intimate relationship in particular, you will notice that, although they may have evolved from previous generations, the basic tenets are pretty much the same as they have always been:

> *"We—you and I—are married or are in a committed relationship. That means you now belong to me, which in turn means that you must fulfill my requirements for feeling important, my sense of belonging, safety, and personal power. You have what I need, and you must give it to me. You are responsible for my happiness and my sense of self."*

Do any of those statements coincide with your beliefs about relationship? If so, you might also recognize that they are fairly universal in nature. The actual words may vary, but the underlying need and sense of incompletion that the words express are shared by almost everyone on the planet. We are like a large flock of sheep, blindly following beliefs about how the need for importance and belonging should be met. Until one leaves the flock, one doesn't even recognize that the needs themselves are simply beliefs and not the Truth!

I wonder if the person who coined the phrase *think outside the box* ever considered that he or she was suggesting we stop using our intellects and turn to our intuition for guidance and inspiration instead. Whether that was the intention, I suggest we use the adage to begin questioning everything we assumed was true about relationship, beginning with the following:

Can the actions or words of another person cause you to feel true happiness?

Let me be clear about the term "true happiness." When I use it, I'm describing an experience that doesn't rely on any conditions in order to exist. Otherwise, we are talking about a feeling that relies on the fulfillment of certain specific conditions, and therefore lasts only as long as those conditions are in place. That kind of happiness is conditional and impermanent and so can't accurately be called true happiness. Unconditional happiness is unconditional, whereas virtually all the goals that we have set for ourselves—spiritual, material, or sentimental—have reinforced a belief that happiness is something that is achieved by meeting certain conditions:

"I can't be happy until I find my one true love. I won't be satisfied with anything less than ten million dollars. How can I feel good when I know so many people are suffering? I can't be at peace until I know my child is financially secure," and so on.

Expectation Overload

When you consider the meaning of unconditional happiness, you come to see that what you have been trying to get from your partner is an impermanent experience, such as relief, affection, reassurance, encouragement, comfort, or physical pleasure, while calling each of these "love." The following two statements are examples of what I have heard in my workshops. On the face of it, they may sound reasonable and undemanding, but upon closer examination you might discover that they are loaded with unspoken expectations:

"I'm not asking for much from my husband; I just want a hug."

"I don't want my wife to make me happy all the time; I just want her to leave me alone and give me some space."

Looking at these one case at a time, the dialogues in question went something like this.

"I'm not asking for much from my husband," said a female participant. "I just want a hug."

"You mean he has never hugged you?" I asked.

"Yes, but he hasn't hugged me much lately."

"But he does hug you sometimes."

"Yes, but he doesn't hug me the right way."

"What's the right way?" I asked.

"I just want him to show me he cares!"

"So how could he hug you to show you he cares?"

"You know what I mean," she insisted. "I want him to show some passion and love!"

"So you don't just want a hug," I said. "You want something more from him."

"Well, he's my husband!"

"And so . . . ?" I urged her, hoping she would explain what a marriage license entitled her to.

"So?!" she replied as if in shock.

Now she was putting me in the same boat as her husband—we were both supposed to be mind readers.

"So he should treat me like his wife! I want to feel that he really *wants* me. I want to know that I am the most important person in his life and that he appreciates all I have given to him."

"And you think he can communicate all that in a hug?"

"Yes!" she said. Then she thought about it. "Well, that would be a good start."

By this point I sensed that she would never be satisfied as long as she was fixated on getting that specific kind of embrace and that, eventually, she would either give up and leave the marriage or stick it out with bitterness, resentment, or resignation. Obviously, the issue involved more than just a hug.

———

Now let's look at the second statement.

"I don't want my wife to make me happy all the time," he said. "I just want her to leave me alone and give me some space."

His arms were folded and he was leaning back in his seat so that the chair's front feet left the floor.

"How much space would you need?" I asked.

"I don't know," he said, "just enough. She's always coming into my office space at home, asking me questions and wanting to talk. I just want her to leave me alone so I can work in peace!"

"So you want her to leave you alone all day, every day?"

"Only when I'm at home in my office," he said.

"I see."

I remained silent for a moment, waiting for what I knew was coming. After a few seconds he spoke again.

"And when I'm watching TV or on the computer."

"Or in bed, or at the supper table . . ." I offered.

"No, we can talk at supper."

"Right, but the rest of the time she should shut up."

"I *never* tell her to shut up," he said (and I considered that I could have used less provocative language). "I'm always respectful to her. But she keeps coming in and interrupting me or asking me if I want to do something with her, and always when I'm really busy!"

"What a coincidence," I said, but he ignored the insinuation.

"I just want her to leave me alone."

"All the time?" I wondered aloud. "What if she *did* leave you alone? What would that mean to you?"

"That she understands me," he said. "And that she respects me."

"Would it also means that she loves you?"

"I don't know." He shrugged noncommittally. "Maybe."

"So if she left you alone all the time, that would prove that she really loved you," I said, and then began to be more playful with the participant. "I suppose, if she walks out and leaves you for good, that means she's crazy about you!"

This drew a laugh from the group.

"And I guess if she moves to another country," I said, "that proves her unconditional love for you!"

"No, I *want* to live with her," he said, leaning farther back in his chair. "I just need to be alone sometimes."

"So you want her around, but not too close. You want her to be available when you need her, but you want her to stay away the rest of the time. And you want her to know when to stay away and when to move closer, is that right?"

This drew a comment from another female participant.

"It sounds like you're talking about his dog!"

Laughs from the others.

As I was writing the above lines, I started to wonder what a marriage would be like for the woman who wanted a hug to be living with the man who wanted to be left alone. The response came immediately to mind—why, it would be like almost every marriage on the planet!

When you believe that your partner holds the key to your happiness and fulfillment, your sense of value will be reflected to you in the actions (or inactions) and words (or silence) of the other. Regarding the first example above, if the woman's husband hugs her, her sense of value will increase temporarily. But it will soon diminish again, and she will need another hug but this time it will have to be a better hug. If it's the same as the last hug, the sense of value will not be as strong, if it appears at all, and disappointment will creep in. The next hug, if it happens at all, will probably be more disappointing, and increasingly she will experience herself as a person of very little value. Of course, she will continue to believe, because of what she is not getting from her husband, that she is a limited, incomplete human being, rather than seeing the magnificent being that is merely pretending to be her.

The husband who wants his space will continue to see his wife as inconsiderate of his needs, and her behavior will reflect his sense of himself as a misunderstood, unappreciated man with unreasonable demands being placed upon him. Being the more independent in the marriage, he will deny that he needs anything from her personally but would no doubt feel extremely uncomfortable if she were to withdraw her attention from him and pursue interests and friendships away from the marriage. Being independent, he is unaware that what he needs is for her to be silently waiting for his attention, as well as for her to express excitement and joy when he deigns to honor her with said attention. Through her patient waiting and visible adoration (Hey, wait a minute, that *does* sound like his dog!), he believes he will be fulfilled. And so he remains unaware of his membership in the flock of those who pursue in others what they think they need in order to feel whole and happy.

The Insatiable Hunger

Dissatisfaction is the driving force behind so many human pursuits. The insatiable nature of need is behind all dissatisfaction, and working in tandem with need is the belief in one's human incompleteness. But what if you are *not* incomplete? What if the truth is that you have been living in a trance of forgetfulness, surrounded by a world that is designed to reinforce your trance until you reach a point where you wake up from the trance and enjoy the experience of remembering what *You*, in fact, are? How would it affect all your relationships if you were to stop looking at others as sources of happiness and the fulfillment of your personal needs? What would it be like to leave the flock and experience relationships beyond belief?

That all sounds really nice—great, even—but it seems unrealistic to me! Down here in the real world, I do feel

> *that I'm incomplete and that I'm missing something. And
> if I can't at least get some of what I need from my partner,
> what's the point of being in a relationship?*

The point is to help you see that you're *not* incomplete and you *don't* need what you already have.

> *But I'm not imagining this sense of incompletion! I'm
> not imagining my needs—they're there, inside me. I'm only
> human, dammit!*

But you're not *only* human, and that sense of incompleteness or need is not as real as you think it is. Let's consider what need is by looking at it as a kind of hunger. Imagine yourself being extremely famished—as hungry as someone who hasn't eaten in three or four days and has no money for food. How do you imagine you would see the world in that case? Personally, I think my mind would be constantly drawn to the object of my hunger—food of any kind! I also imagine that I would look at people as a means to getting that food and focus on the one that seemed to promise the greatest chance of success. Next, I would have to consider how I could get food from that person, which is where manipulation comes in. I would have to speak and act in ways that would inspire, encourage, coerce, or even threaten the person to give me food. Of course, I would be humble and inoffensive at first, perhaps even charming and humorous. If that type of behavior did not produce the desired nourishment, I would have to resort to more assertive, even aggressive, means. If I had enough strength I might even physically intimidate the other person—perhaps even overwhelm them physically—in order to achieve my goal. Ultimately, I would either get what I hungered for or give up in defeat and go looking elsewhere for my survival.

When you read the preceding example, did you see the similarities between the physical need for food and the emotional need for love and happiness? Both needs cause one to see others as sources of fulfillment. You might say that both needs cause one to see others as the means to success or disappointment. Both needs inspire one to try to figure out a way to control and manipulate another person into giving what one believes one needs in order to survive and flourish.

Yes, and both need and hunger are a part of my being human. And if I don't get the food—from somewhere outside of me—I will die! If I don't get love from my partner I will—

—have to look to where it actually exists! You believe you are in a relationship to get your needs met when, in fact, your relationship has a far more important purpose than making you feel special. It is helping you wake up and remember that—

—I know, I know, remember that happiness is inside of me, and that I have to make myself happy and love myself, et cetera, et cetera . . .

Well, not quite. This is more about waking up and remembering that *You* are in a constant state of True Happiness—you're already complete—but have forgotten that and are believing the opposite. When you believe you're incomplete, then your needs take over and drive you to look to the world for your fulfillment.

Where need is involved, nothing is ever neutral. When you look at the world through the eyes of need, everything becomes intensely personal. If your partner forgets your birthday, and you need him/her to prove that you are special by celebrating your birthday enthusiastically, you will interpret your partner's forgetfulness as evidence that he/she is withholding love from you. If your partner remembers, but doesn't celebrate it with the enthusiasm you feel you need, you will again interpret his/her behavior as a dismissal of your importance and believe that he/she is purposely withholding from you what you have every right to be given. When it comes to the need to feel special, *everything* is personal!

Many of us enter a relationship with expectations that our partners will provide the proof that we are special individuals. But what happens when that proof is not forthcoming and our need for importance goes unsatisfied?

To answer that question, let's go a step further with the belief that someone else is your source of true happiness. As stated earlier, thinking someone has to make you happy tends to reinforce the belief that you are not happy yet and thus are incomplete. Most people don't like feeling incomplete and tend to believe there is something wrong with them. That guilty assumption often causes people to think they are undeserving, and so must *earn, prove, or claim* the right to happiness. This is where manipulation comes in. Manipulations in relationships tend to be clever forms of behavior and speech, designed to induce a loving response from one's partner. You could never come right out and beg your partner to make you happy because that would reveal the raw vulnerability of your need, which you see as repulsive. Therefore, you must resort to behaviors you created in your childhood and made more sophisticated as you grew up. Since I can't list all the individual behaviors that human beings express, I have generalized and encapsulated as many as I could into some basic examples. I also generalized about the order in which these manipulations appear in a relationship.

Earning Love and Happiness From Your Partner

The difference between earning and proving your right is so subtle they are almost indistinguishable. The way I am using the terms simply denotes the degree of apparent confidence with which the need is expressed. If you attempt to earn your way to happiness, your approach would often seem to be more passive. You will go out of your way to do more for your partner than your partner seems to be doing for you. You will sacrifice your career, your friends, and even your family in order to be available to your partner's whims and needs. You will always feel that you must contribute more to the relationship than your partner is contributing because you are compensating for the sense that you are incomplete and, therefore, less deserving. You will make yourself available to be your partner's companion whenever he/she has the time or the desire to be with you. Sometimes you will apply a great deal of energy, using playfulness, sexual allure, or enthusiasm in order to get your partner's attention and draw him/her into a greater level of engagement with the relationship.

Of course, you can always turn to one of the favorite relationship pastimes and simply complain about your partner's lack of attention to—or involvement with—the partnership after ensuring that you have done enough in the recent past to justify your right to the complaints.

Another approach that sometimes seems to work (but never

actually brings true happiness) is to try to make your partner jealous. This does not necessarily require that you flirt with, or display a strong attraction to, another individual in front of your partner. The key is to pretend to put more of your attention in a direction away from your partner. An especially good ploy is to praise someone else about a characteristic that your partner associates with him/herself. For instance, if your partner likes to make others laugh, talk about so-and-so and what a wonderful sense of humor they have. If your partner is invested in his/her appearance, simply remark on how attractive so-and-so is, or what a great body so-and-so has. You might passively suggest your admiration for the way so-and-so expresses their affection toward their partner. Or else you can pour yourself into a personal interest or pastime, creating the appearance of wanting it more than you want your partner. Pretending not to need him/her is often a very effective way of grabbing their attention and getting your partner to pursue you. Getting happiness from your partner is hard work and demands a lot of your time and energy, but you will believe it's worth the investment since you're convinced that your partner is your source of happiness and love. And it's okay to enjoy the results, regardless of how temporary the feelings are because, remember, you earned it!

Proving Your Right To Getting Love and Happiness From Your Partner

To prove that you have the right to be happy and loved, and that your partner must give these to you, you have to become your own publicist. First of all, you must convince yourself that you are the perfect mate, or at the very least, a much better mate than your partner is proving to be. Once you've accomplished this, you can go about advertising all the things you are doing in the name of satisfying your partner. When you want something from him/her, make sure that they are aware of all the ways you have proven your love for them, employing exaggeration when and as needed. It's always good to make your partner see that what you are asking of them is much less than what you are giving on a daily basis. "I do all of these things for you, and all I ask in return is one little thing!" is the standard refrain here. Also, in preparing to make your request known, make sure you let your partner know every little thing you have just done for them, such as—

"I picked up that package for you, honey."

"I made you a cup of tea, just the way you like it,
sweetheart."

"Mother invited us over on Sunday, darling, but I
made up an excuse because I know you wanted
to play golf this weekend."

"That scarf I bought you looks great on you,
sweetheart! How do you like it?"

"I took off from work early so I could come home
and take care of you, my love. How is that flu
treating you?"

After making your partner aware of each thing you did on his/her behalf, you can then list them all again whenever your partner hesitates in fulfilling your request for that tiny display of love you require.

Another manner in which you can prove that you deserve the love and happiness your partner should be giving you (*freely* if they really loved you) is to incite a feeling of jealousy in them. In this case you have to attract attention to yourself that proves your desirability, which may involve actually flirting with other men or women in front of your partner, praising or bragging about ex-partners, or disclosing experiences of men or women coming on to you. The attention that you draw to yourself does not necessarily have to be sexual (although it certainly doesn't hurt matters), as long as you can get the spotlight on yourself and draw compliments and admiration from others. This will prove to your partner what a valuable asset you are to them and thus urge or inspire them to behave in ways that make you feel loved and happy!

Claiming Your Right to Have Love and Happiness From Your Partner

This is a more aggressive approach, and it's generally used when the previous two methods don't bring about the expected results. Claiming your right to get love and happiness from your partner may involve you bringing out the so-called "Relationship Rule Book," an old code of behavior, the origins of which are unknown to any of us. This book includes the idea that you and your partner are in an exclusive and special relationship, rendering you to be each other's property.

(Note: There are cases of the rule book being a one-way code that is heavily in favor of the husband in a heterosexual relationship, where most of the laws concern how the woman should behave in order to ensure the man's happiness and contentment. For the purposes of *this* book, I am referring to a code that is somewhat more balanced, and is designed to govern both partners, regardless of gender.)

When you want your partner to make you happy, you can simply pull out the rule book and tell them how they should be behaving. The Relationship Rule Book gives you the right to demand that your expectations be fulfilled. After all, that's why you are in this relationship, isn't it? If the purpose is not to make you happy, why even be together? And to justify your demands even more strongly, you can always remind them:

"You're *my* partner! You're supposed to love me! You're supposed to make me feel more important than anyone or anything else!"

And if this doesn't work, you have the right to threaten your partner with some form of punishment—including desertion—unless they start fulfilling their commitment to the partnership.

Demands, threats, criticisms, ultimatums . . . these are the tools you can use to claim your right to the happiness your partner is withholding from you, all justified in the handy Relationship Rule Book. The fact that nobody possesses the actual book (and if they did they could not possibly read the entire tome) does not stop us from referring to it whenever we see our partners as the source of our happiness and perceive them to be withholding it from us.

Another approach you can use is to make your partner jealous by having an affair. This is like making a bold statement (using skywriting) that informs your partner that you are claiming your right to get happiness from outside yourself, and if your partner is denying your claim, then you're damn well going to get it from a more willing source.

(Notice that I included "make your partner jealous" in *all* the approaches I described. This is because, come on, how much fun would relationships be if we couldn't make the other person jealous?)

I hope that you realized I was taking a tongue in cheek approach when describing these various manipulations. I learned a long time ago that none of these approaches actually work, no matter how often they're employed. As a matter of fact, what little effectiveness they may seem to have had in the beginning stages of your relationship wears thin pretty fast. After a while, your attempts to manipulate your partner into *loving* you (i.e., making you feel special) will most often be met with resistance, resentment, and rejection.

The central theme to all these approaches is the belief that you are not the source of your happiness and so must look outward for it, ultimately making your partner an essential source. However, your relationship is only reflecting back to you a belief and attitude that permeates every aspect of your life. The belief is that you are an incomplete being, with the potential, one hopes, to become whole at some point in the future (if you live long enough). The attitude is that you must interact with the world in certain ways in order to gain that completeness from *out there.*

In simple terms, if you're not happy, you believe that it's because there is no happiness inside you. Therefore, you reason, you must come up with a plan and an approach to find that happiness outside and draw it into you.

The Happiness Train

Figure 1.1

In this model (Figure 1.1), you might see a number of areas where you have specific or vague goals. Perhaps you want a

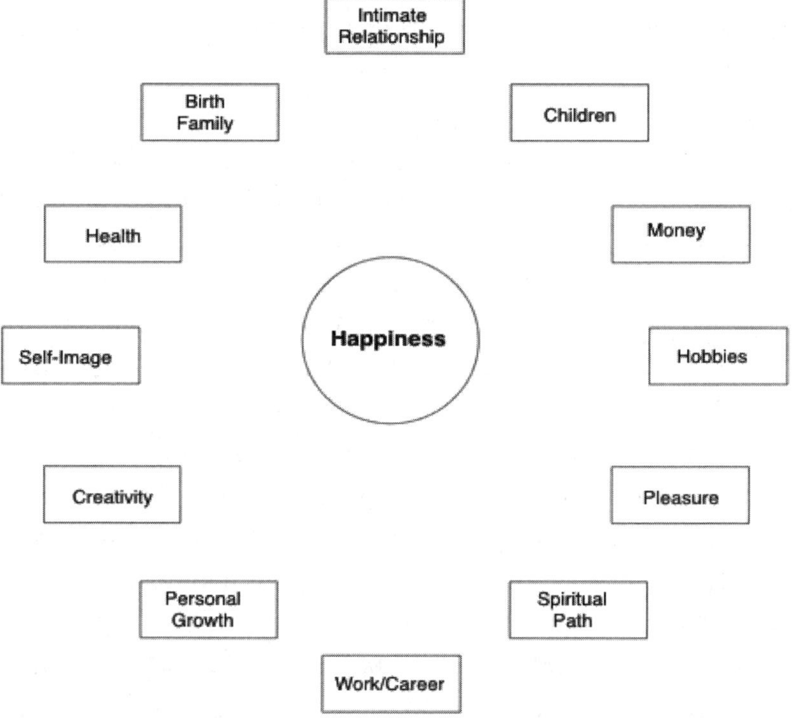

healthy body that will carry you well into your nineties and beyond. Or maybe there's an old emotional trauma that you want to heal, an amount of money you wish to possess, a spiritual experience you read about and want to have for yourself, and so forth. But have you looked at what you will experience when that goal is reached?

Typically, we want to reach those goals so that we can experience something that is beyond our fears, anxieties, and pains—something that you might call *happiness.* You are striving to reach what you consider important goals in your life, but surely you recognize that the goals themselves are not the purpose of your efforts. You want the experience that you believe will come with the attainments or achievements represented by the goals. If you look again at Figure 1.1, imagine that each of those boxes is a train car, and that the train was designed to take you to that one destination called Happiness. While that may have been the original idea for this Happiness Train, you might also notice the train is on a circular track, surrounding its supposed destination, but never actually getting there.

I was on that train ride to happiness for most of my life. All my material pursuits, spiritual practices, psychological explorations, and philosophical studies emerged from the hopeful fantasy that perhaps if I was spiritual enough and I served humankind and I practiced being a truly decent human being and I drank good whiskey and had as much sex as possible and had lots of money and my children were happy and successful and my wife and I loved each other forever and—let's see . . . *oh!*—and I healed all my old subconscious wounds and was a successful workshop leader and . . . *whew!* I'm getting tired just listing all of them! But anyway, I believed that if I fulfilled all those goals, the train would bring me to its destination and I could finally be permanently happy. And I had to reach *all* of the goals; otherwise, I could not be happy at all.

But one day I jumped off (or more likely fell off) the Happiness Train and realized what a man had told me when I was twenty years old:

"Everybody thinks that they need some *thing* to make them happy. The truth is that only *happiness* makes you happy!"

It took me more than thirty years to understand what the hell he meant.

Whether my goals were purely fantasies of the *if-only* persuasion; solid, attainable prizes; or imminently achievable events, the desire to reach those goals is always oriented toward the future. But happiness can only be experienced in the moment. It is always available and free of charges or conditions, and that's a good thing since the future never comes and it's always *now*.

> *But if it's always available right now, why am I not experiencing it? What do I have to do so I can feel that happiness constantly?*

Well, you might start by confronting the belief that happiness is a good feeling.

> *What? You mean happiness doesn't feel good? That's crazy!*

Happiness is not a feeling at all. It's there when you're feeling good or bad. If you confine the experience of happiness only to times when you're feeling good, then you will ignore its existence when discomfort arises in you. You might observe your partner behaving in a certain way and begin to feel irritated. At that point you are not feeling *good*, so you become more focused on *bad* feelings. Since you believe that you can't be happy when you're feeling bad, you react to your partner's behavior as if it's the cause of your bad feelings and strive for a solution that will make you feel good again. You will try to change your partner's present behavior or appearance into one that makes you feel better. Thus, your partner becomes your source of happiness. But it's not real happiness you are striving for because, as I suggested, true happiness can't be earned, bought, or coerced into existence. It's just *there,* so to speak. What you are striving for is an *idea* of happiness that is based on feeling good.

> *But I like feeling good! And I only like being around people who make me feel good and doing things that make me feel good.*

Then you will never be truly content. Honestly, when you start chasing after something, you are usually experiencing the opposite. I thought happiness was a conditional experience. I thought if my wife treated me a certain way, it would make me happy. If my children did well in school and had lots of great friends, I would be happy—and so would they. So I tried to control my world and create conditions that would bring me happiness.

Maybe it's the same with you. Maybe you have a big, important goal in your life, and you don't want to hear me saying it will not make you happy. I guarantee that the goal will not make you truly happy, but maybe you just want to believe that it is absolutely essential to your life. Maybe you just want your partner to change. You don't want to hear that it's possible to be happy even while your partner remains exactly as he or she is right now. But the happiness I'm talking about—*true happiness*—is not dependent on anything; it doesn't need anything. I'm experiencing it right now, and it's not asking anything of me in return—it doesn't even care if I'm aware of it or not!

I once read an article about a group of scientists in America who were studying happiness. They approached two men, one who had just won the lottery and another who had just been in an accident and was paralyzed from the waist down. It seemed obvious to those performing the study that the paralyzed man was not as happy as the lottery winner, but one year later they visited the two men and discovered that both men were at the same level of happiness and contentment—not a very high level either, by the way. The truth is that happiness, love, peace, and joy cannot be bound by conditions. True happiness is always present. And if that is true, then it's also true that *you* are that happiness because whenever you become aware of the present moment, there you are! Goals are in the future. Happiness is in the now. If you are not aware of it, and don't know *how* to be aware of it, this book can be of assistance to you as you read on.

Love? Really?

Among all the areas listed in what I called *The Happiness Train*, there is an idea that is held to be true by the majority of people all over the world. Even more prevalent than the belief that money is the key to happiness is the belief that true happiness can be experienced once you find that special someone— that *one true love*. I spent twenty-five years of my life trying to help people to have happy marriages and consistently heard the message that one's partner must be responsible for instilling happiness. It becomes apparent in the romantic stage, with statements such as

- "I can't live without you."

- "You complete me."

- "There is no me without you."

- "You are my soul mate."

- "You're the meaning and inspiration in my life."

- "You are the one I have been searching for my whole life."

- "There is no point in going on without you."

As I was writing the lines above, I had this humorous image of greeting the postman at the door and saying, "You complete me." Then the scene extended to me walking down the street and greeting people with similar sentiments. People would probably think I was crazy, wouldn't they? But picking one person out of the billions of people in the world and professing those sentiments? Well, *that's* not crazy at all—that's love! However, when you think about it, you see that the sentiment you are expressing is so rife with conditions and expectations that only someone immersed in the trance of forgetting who they really are could see that as love.

When you search for that one true love, you're looking for someone who can make you feel happy *forever*! Thus, you form a special bond with the other person, thinking that the feeling of specialness is the same as true happiness. Now that person's job is to constantly make you feel special. If your partner makes you feel special, then your partner loves you. If you are loved, then you are happy. If your partner does not make you feel special, then you are not loved and, therefore, cannot be happy. Let me paraphrase what the marriage expert David Schnarch has often said: Relationship is not about love; it's about importance.

So now we come to the crux of the relationship phenomenon. People enter all relationships with the belief that the other person is responsible for *all* of their feelings, and that their partner has the capacity to make them feel good all the time if their partner so chooses. Meanwhile the partner enters the relationship with the exact same agenda. Now you have two people echoing one sentiment: "You are mine now. You hold the key to my happiness, and my role is to wait for you to give it to me. While I wait, I will either earn, prove, or claim my right to the happiness and love that you now owe me."

But wait a minute! Your goals and intentions in the relationship are not really about love and happiness; your focus is on being made to feel special! You want your partner to build you up with admiration, gratitude, praise, unflagging encouragement, devotion, and dedication. You want your partner to brag about you to others and talk about what a perfectly wonderful companion you are—so wise, intelligent, attractive, and erotically gifted. And you want this input to be as constant as the rising sun.

When your partner does seem to be supporting feelings of importance and belonging in you, you feel an expansive sensation in your body that you *believe to be* happiness, love, peace, fulfillment, et cetera, but it's not any of those. It's the temporary expansive sensation of personal importance or *specialness*. And temporary is not real or true.

There's a Hole in My Bucket

Before we close this chapter, let's look at one more aspect of the quest for happiness in which we allow our relationships to play a key part. Consider the motivating force behind your thirst for fulfillment. The most logical assumption would be that it would be that a lack of fulfillment initiates the desire and subsequent search for fulfillment; unhappiness makes you want to be happy; absence of love drives you to find love. This sense of lack seems to produce specific tendencies in you that dominate almost all aspects of your life. Let's call these tendencies *obsession, fixation, compulsion,* and *addiction.*

Obsession is an emotional preoccupation that seems to have its roots in anxiety. Some people are more overt than others when they express an obsession, and some display outright obsessive personalities, but every human being becomes obsessive at various points in their lives because it's a characteristic of the human entity. You certainly don't see animals caught in a state of angst concerning how they might look in the eyes of others of their species. And even though chipmunks do look like they're in a constant state of panic, especially when they're eating, studies have not revealed the presence of any kind of fear in animals unless they are in a very real danger of being physically hurt or killed. Humans, on the other hand, can experience panic when the danger is purely an imagined one.

Where obsession appears to be an emotional state, fixation seems more mental, and compulsion is a behavioral expression of one's humanness. Addiction is physical and has appeared in other primates. Of course, it could be argued that all four aspects appear in the animal community, but this might only be because we are aware of them in ourselves and so can project our nature while attempting to interpret the behaviors of other species. But back to the point of all this.

Obsession, fixation, compulsion, and addiction all seem to have the same source—a sense of lacking in the human being, and the need that expresses this perceived lack. Therefore, as long as you need something from your partner (such as a sense of importance), you are prone to falling into patterns of fixation, obsession, and/or compulsion. On the outside, that might look like falling into repetitive patterns of speech and behavior that may hide the rawness and vulnerability of your need but will rarely, if ever, produce the results you are seeking. This is because (a) the need can *never* be completely satisfied—not even anywhere near completely—and (b) importance is not true happiness. At best it's a temporary facsimile of happiness, love, and fulfillment.

Need is like an empty cup that symbolizes the belief that you are incomplete and, therefore, lacking. Through compulsive behaviors, you may go around trying to get people to fill your cup with appreciation, gratitude, admiration, praise, encouragement, et cetera. And on those occasions that they actually *do* express your importance to them, you may feel sated with elation and what passes for *love*. But that too will pass because, if you look at the bottom of your cup, you'll see that it's actually a sieve through which the good feeling drains away. Pretty soon you will be back to your unconscious, compulsive patterns of behavior and will perpetuate the patterns up to the point where you wake up and realize that your true nature and being is a constant state of pure, unconditional happiness and that there is no love to be had *out there*.

This leads to the summary points of this chapter:

- When you are in any kind of emotionally committed relationship, your partner becomes the source of fulfillment concerning your needs for importance and belonging.

- You have specific, even predictable, forms of behavior designed to get those needs met.

- The behaviors are carried out, typically, without any awareness whatsoever on your part.

- The compulsive behaviors are childish—they were formed in early childhood and later disguised with a more adult-like appearance and sophistication.

- Bringing awareness to your behavior will ultimately shine a light on the insatiability of your needs and help you see the futility of trying to get those needs permanently fulfilled by a partner or anyone or *anything* else in the world, be it money, achievements, gurus, friends, fans, or whatever you care to believe.

CHAPTER 2

Pride, Prejudice, and Process

Principle #2: My partner is not the cause of my unhappiness or pain.

THERE ARE A LOT OF THEORIES concerning how we came to be here in this world and in this physical body we call human. Mythology, philosophy, religion, and science each have their explanations and forms of logic to support their hypotheses, and we are all free to dismiss some and favor others. Bottom line: You are in a human body and are likely to have many of the experiences that condition includes. Whether your ancient ancestors climbed down from the trees or simply appeared on the planet, there is evidence that they found shelter in caves, built fires and wore animal skins for warmth, invented tools to make basic survival easier, and strove to bring more comfort into their lives. Why? Because there is a great deal of discomfort in being human. As much as other animals have been able to adapt to their environments, human beings never seemed to have quite gotten the hang of it, and we have continued on our restless way, never really finding that point where we could say, "Whew! We made it! Now we can relax."

Physical, emotional, and possibly mental discomforts seem to be our lot in life. In human existence, pain is a given, or at least it has been up to this point in our history, as it has been in the animal realms. But along with pain, there seem to be a number of tendencies that are particular to the human experience, two of these being our tendency to suffer and the tendency to blame someone or something for the cause of our pain and suffering. First, I would like to briefly delineate the difference between pain and suffering. I define pain as any basic form of discomfort on the physical or emotional/feeling levels (we'll talk about the difference between feelings and emotions later, as well). Suffering is the emotional reaction to pain that is due to our rejection of the discomfort. Suffering is the opposite of peaceful acceptance.

When you reject your discomfort, you will typically look for two things: an explanation for *why* you are experiencing this state (which includes who or what is behind the why) and *how* you can make the pain stop. The rational mind cannot think outside the boundaries of cause and effect. If you have a stomach ache, it must be due to something else—something you ate, perhaps. If you have a headache, there must be an outside influence that initially caused it. If you are sad, some event must have caused its existence. Even DNA is considered an outside originator of your physical, emotional, or mental predispositions (after all, it's not exactly *your* DNA, but rather an ancestral construct that you were burdened with at conception) along with some other trigger to initiate the experience of pain. So,

"Why is it here and how do I fix it?" These questions become your default position whenever pain surfaces in your awareness. And that is pretty much why you will blame your partner for a great deal of your discomfort in the relationship.

If you notice yourself feeling unhappy while witnessing your partner's behavior, you will likely think that that behavior must be the *cause* of your unhappiness. After all, you did previously let them know what you liked and didn't like, and yet there your partner is, deliberately pissing you off by acting or speaking in a way you don't like! It's simply a matter of one plus one equaling two. *Your partner's behavior + Your irritation = It's your partner's fault!* And two plus two equals four, as well. *Your partner ceases that behavior + You feel better = See, it was your partner's fault!* You have just scientifically and mathematically proven that your partner can be the cause of your unhappiness. And since this is the obvious truth, you can justify your anger, as well as your demand that your partner changes. So, regarding the previous question of, "Why is it here, and how can I fix it?" the answer seems pretty simple:

> *The pain is here because my partner caused it to appear in my body, and it gets fixed by my partner apologizing and then changing.*

Sure, you've felt that irritation and discomfort in the past, but it was *always* because someone else made you feel it, and now your partner makes you feel it even more deeply than you have since you were a child, when Mom or Dad would do something to make you feel unloved, unwanted, or unimportant.

But what if discomfort is actually no one's fault? Not your partner's, not Mom or Dad's, not the government's . . . what if no one is ever to blame because no one can cause pain in another individual?

> *I don't know about that. What if someone comes up and hits me on the head with a hammer? I'd say they were the cause of my pain! And if someone can do that on a physical level, why can't they be capable of hurting me emotionally?*

For now, let's just focus on emotional discomfort. Regarding emotional adulthood, in my life as a husband, father, son, counselor, and in all my relationships, I have never witnessed anyone being the cause of my emotional discomfort.

I know this may sound crazy, but what if you experience pain simply because you are human and pain is part of the human journey? Maybe it will not be with you for the entire duration of the journey—however long that is—but thus far, pain seems to be one of the things all people have in common. Not only do we all feel pain, but in fact, we all feel the exact same pain! You may react to loneliness differently than I do, and you may describe the feeling in different words, but loneliness is loneliness, isn't it? And although it's common for people to believe that loneliness is a feeling that only occurs in certain circumstances, that doesn't mean the circumstances are the actual cause of the feeling. Maybe we can look at the subject of feelings from a different point of view, one that can help free us from the compulsion of playing the so-called blame game. As you read the following explanation, I encourage you to listen to your heart in order to determine whether the words point to the Truth.

First, consider that you existed before you were born into this human form; that there was a *You* before there was a you. It would be impossible for anyone to accurately describe to you who and what *You* really are, since language (and vocabulary) is a human design, created to enhance human experiences and beliefs. What *You* are is far beyond human, and so I use the word *ineffable*, and one of its dictionary meanings: "too great and beautiful to be described." How and why the ineffable *You* decided to take on the traits and physical limitations of a human being is something that can never be understood by the human intellect, except perhaps in a very abstract manner or through metaphors. But let's just say that, in *Your* infinite wisdom, love, intelligence, creative imagination, and power, *You* came into this world where you could have the imaginary experience of being human.

Now, consider that *You* are a being that does not experience duality. *You* are whole and indivisible, unlimited by the illusory confines of time and space. Importantly, for the sake of this explanation, *You* do not experience pain. Then *You,* through *Your* free will and unlimited creative power, create the phenomenon of being human, which is the precise opposite of what *You* are. As a human being, you experience all aspects of duality—separation, limitation, unconsciousness, fear, and guilt, as well as the so-called positive experiences of elation, affection, confidence, forgiveness, and so on. And you experience pain, for no particular reason, other than that pain is part of the human experience. Nobody did this to *You*; it's an experience of *Your* choosing and creation. As the person that you think you are, you are free to blame anyone and everyone, including God, for all the problems, limitations, and discomforts you face in your life. You can even blame your essence or soul for falling from grace, sinning, or turning your back on God, but that is only because you are unaware that *You* wanted a completely *human* experience.

As part of the human journey, the word "forgiveness" is introduced to you as a way to free yourself from the burden of the pain someone else supposedly caused you. The problem with forgiveness is that it's so damn hard, and the forgiveness process takes so long to complete. I know of people that have been trying to forgive their parents for decades and still feel they have plenty more work to do. I tried forgiving my father for more than thirty years, all the while considering that, once I was finished with Dad, I still had Mom to contend with!

What about you and your partner? Are there some events in your life that your partner seemed to engineer and for which you can't forgive them yet? Are there certain things you think your partner is capable of doing that you could never forgive? Are you keeping your partner at a safe distance to ensure that you can't get hurt by him/her? Do you keep secrets or leave things unspoken because you don't want to be the unforgivable cause of your partner's pain? It's interesting to me how much humanity suffers while believing that someone else is the cause of the suffering, when in fact it's blame that's the actual cause and forgiveness simply supports the misery.

What!? Forgiveness is part of the problem?

I know that's an outrageous statement to make. However, pain can exist without blame, but forgiveness would not come into our minds at all without first the appearance of blame (including self-blame). So isn't it possible that blame and for-giveness are two sides of the same coin? And since blame is an expression of guilt either toward yourself or toward others, wouldn't a more valuable response be to deal with the guilt directly rather than taking a more circular route of blame and forgiveness, which never confronts the central issue of your human pain anyway? Well, in order to do that, it may be help-ful to take a conscious look at your anger first.

Fire in the Hole!

During a typical unconscious (or caterpillar) stage of the human journey, behaviors are generally compulsive in nature, mean-ing no awareness is involved in your actions or words or even your thoughts. One of the most glaring examples of uncon-scious, compulsive behavior is anger. People almost never enjoy being angry, nor do they plan on being angry. Imagine that you and your partner have just spent a great day out together at the beach or the park and, on the drive back, you are having a pleas-ant conversation. Now imagine that, while you're getting closer to your home, you say to yourself, *I feel really great! As soon as we get in the door, I'm going to start criticizing my partner about leaving the stove burner on, and then I'll really blow up at my partner for for-getting to turn off the lights in the bathroom!* It's not likely that you would think like that but, sure enough, within two minutes of arriving home, you notice the stove burner has been left on, and the wonderful day you had together is obliterated by the ensu-ing explosion of anger.

To complicate matters more, anger can be experienced in other ways that are not so obvious as the explosive nature of outright attack. Maybe your anger is more of an *implosion,* causing you to withdraw from your partner and maintain a stony silence. The emotion churns away inside you, inciting resentful, bitter thoughts that weave a story about how your partner thoughtlessly wronged you. The anger will not allow for hurt to be acknowledged unless it is used to fuel its resentment and bitterness. Meanwhile, your partner is being exposed to a full dose of exclusion, which has often been used as a form of punishment, reaching back to early tribal days. While aggressive attack can be seen as the most honest, the silent treatment or withdrawal is often considered the cruelest expression of anger.

On the other hand, the most deceptive form of anger is expressed as passive aggression. If your anger is expressed passive-aggressively, you will seem on the surface to be less affected than you actually are on the inside. Thus, you will communicate your unhappiness through sharp, sarcastic remarks or teasing. When your partner reacts hurtfully to your words, you will lightly brush off your partner's reaction by insisting that you were only kidding and that they shouldn't take things so personally. This has the quadruple benefit of (1) making your partner look petty and overly sensitive, while (2) getting in a few gleeful jabs that help vent your anger, (3) denying the presence of any anger, and (4) not having to deal with your own hurt feelings. In all three types of anger—aggression, withdrawal, and passive-aggression—avoiding pain is the overall objective.

Pop Quiz

Without thinking too much, respond to the questions below in less than ten words:

- What does your partner do that usually irritates you?

- How do you usually react to the irritation?

- What do you do that usually irritates your partner?

- How does your partner usually react to the irritation?

Generally speaking, people do not consciously choose to be angry and are often unaware of what they are feeling even when they have been in the grip of their rage. Some people can stew for days without confronting themselves or the feelings that are stirring beneath their ill temper, and many occasions, when their emotions are pointed out to them, people will react with statements such as, "I am *not* angry, I'm just really disappointed!" But they won't be feeling the disappointment, heartbreak, sadness, sense of exclusion, valuelessness, or whatever hurt that is actually at the heart of the matter because anger is designed to protect people from their discomfort and to keep them focused on the *story*—that is, what's wrong, why it's happening, and who or what must change in order to resolve the crisis.

Figure 2.1 (on the following page) is a basic diagram that shows where anger usually resides in people. You will notice that when you are angry, your shoulders may tighten and rise, your jaw may tense, your voice may become more strained, and your breathing may be shallow. You might also notice that when you are

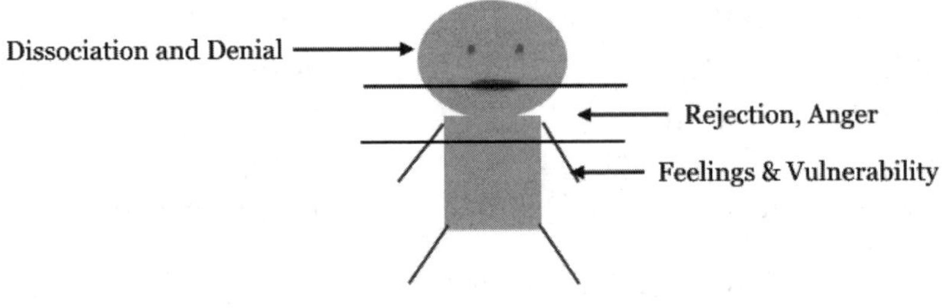

Figure 2.1

feeling sad, anxious, guilty, or other uncomfortable feelings, the experience is entered in some part of your torso, in your heart area or lower. Of course, we don't really *feel* in our heart, except perhaps on a purely physical level. The rejection mechanism seems to be situated just above heart level and acts as a barrier that pushes feelings down and out of your awareness while forcing your attention upward to where your intellect and reason seem to function. More important, the mechanism keeps your attention *outward,* away from your vulnerability, like a thick-walled city that has all of its guns pointed outward to stave off the enemy when, in fact, the real threat is already inside the city walls!

If understanding nurtures growth in awareness, perhaps it would be helpful to explore anger more deeply in order to understand its nature and purpose. It seems that anger is a primal energy that was originally created to protect you from being hurt. As part of the fight-or-flight instinct, anger would be activated whenever an animal was physically threatened and flight was impossible. The interesting thing about human beings is that (a) they can react with anger if physically threatened, but will also do so if they are emotionally threatened; and (b) people can get angry even if the threat is only *imagined*. There have been innumerable cases of people taking offense to something they misheard someone else say. As a matter of fact, a large percentage of anger-infused conflicts are due to misunderstandings over what one person incorrectly assumed or imagined the other said or intended with their behavior.

We will use a fictitious couple, John and Mary, to illustrate, in the points that follow the pattern that the anger dynamic generally follows (John is an app designer who works out of his home office and Mary is a real estate agent):

- Mary is on her way home after working late for the third night in a row.

- John is anxious and somewhat irritated as he tucks their twin daughters into bed after reading them a story.

- As he waits for Mary, he flicks through channels on the television, not really paying attention to what's on. He is thinking about how Mary seems to be paying more attention to her work than to her children. At first he is unaware that this is really about him and that he is feeling abandoned and ignored, but as he considers her effects on the entire family, his anger continues to grow unconsciously.

- An inner monologue takes place in John's head, the words of which serve to justify and intensify his anger: *She hardly sees the children anymore, she's always so busy. And good luck in the sex department! I can't remember the last time we made love—she's always so tired and distracted. Maybe she's got something going at work with that jerk of a boss! Shit! How could she do that to the kids? If I had known she was going to be like this, I would never have agreed to have children. She's so goddamn selfish and irresponsible, and she never even asks about my work or even how the girls are doing in school! I don't even know her anymore!* As he keeps flicking through the channels, he continues to criticize and judge his wife's behavior, until she finally appears and is met by the look of cold disdain on her husband's face. When she asks what's wrong, he snaps a bitter "Nothing!" and stomps off to bed.

- After a lousy night's sleep, John remains cold and silent toward Mary the next day, and the day after, and the day after . . . All the while, John listens to the same monologue in his head about what a selfish, irresponsible mother and wife Mary is until they have a big weekend blowup, filled with accusations, defensive reactions, attacks, and counterattacks. Mary insists she is working overtime to support the family, and John insists that she is abandoning that same family to pursue her own desires.

- There is another day or two of silence interspersed with cautious dialogue.

- A truce is formed as they find safe topics to discuss. For now, the anger has run its course, driven a wedge between John and Mary, and established a new distance that they can maintain, as long as they tread carefully.

- John privately concedes that they do need the money since his job does not pay enough to support the family and although he is resentful, he tolerates Mary's late hours—for now . . .

Although the stories vary according to the participating characters, the basic steps that follow are almost universal in all relationships:

- John is unaware that an old hurt feeling of unimportance is surfacing in him.

- His defense system automatically rejects the hurt, and John feels irritated.

- John mentally searches for the cause of the irritation.

- His mind latches on to Mary's behavior.

- John now thinks Mary's behavior is the cause of his discontent.

- His irritation grows into anger toward his wife.

- John uses the children to justify his perception of Mary as the bad guy and begins to search for ways to change her behavior.

- John enters into a power struggle with Mary.

- Eventually, a cautious truce is formed. Mary is still the bad guy but John has found a compromise in himself that gives him a certain degree of ease.

- The old pain of insignificance that had attempted to

surface has gone temporarily dormant or has driven him to get his sense of importance from his children or work.

The Three Doorways

You may be interested to note that steps 1 through 8 in the preceding John-and-Mary analysis all occurred in less than one minute and that John was in the power-struggle state well before Mary even appeared. John had no idea what old hurt was beginning to surface in him. All he knew was that he was unhappy, that Mary was the cause, and that he felt justified in his anger and judgment of her. In fact, I wonder if John was even aware that he was unhappy. So many of us do not stop to face our internal workings at all and live in a state of constant reaction to outside or physical stimuli. A great first step would have been for John to recognize what exactly he was feeling. It's very simple to do this because underneath every relationship problem that causes us irritation or anxiety you will find three human experiences, one of which may be more obvious than the other two:

Abandonment—Unworthiness—Heartbreak

The experiences connected to abandonment include feeling afraid, lonely, lost, isolated, excluded, not belonging, unwanted, and desolate, among others.

When unworthiness surfaces, people often express feelings of guilt, failure, inadequacy, insignificance, unimportance, valuelessness, stupidity, burdensomeness, or uselessness, among others.

Heartbreak is a profoundly sad experience associated with

crushing disappointment, loss, despair, helplessness, hopelessness, or feeling betrayed, among others.

When you are in a situation that you believe is causing you discomfort, I can assure you that abandonment and/or unworthiness and/or heartbreak are at play behind the scenes. I can also assure you that you had those feelings inside you before that situation ever arose. The worst that one can say about the situation is that it's acting as a catalyst to help you be aware of those feelings, but I prefer to see the situation merely as a neutral event that *reflects* your internal experience. It's a mirror, poised to look inward. A mirror is empty in and of itself, reflecting anything that is put in front of it, and if you are judging what you see in that mirror, well, the mirror will reflect the judgment as well.

The Human Experience

All situations are neutral. That is one of the most difficult statements I have ever had to face. It took me years to see the truth in those words because I wanted so much for something outside myself to be responsible for all the unhappiness and misery I perceived in the world (and in me too, of course). And if the world was, in fact, neither good nor bad, how could I explain what I was seeing? I was convinced that sometimes people did things that made me unhappy, and my logical, rational mind completely supported my perceptions—except when it told me it was my own stupidity, weakness, inadequacy, and overall *wrongness* that were causing my misery (but we'll get to that part later).

As I grow in consciousness, I see more clearly that no one is to blame for my unhappiness and that my wife is simply a wonderful mirror that helps me to see what is blocking my awareness of the *magnificence that I truly am*. The pain that I used to believe she caused me is actually a dynamic component of the belief system that blinds me to the truth. Let me explain as simply as I can.

You begin your human existence in the same way everyone else does, entering this virtual, multidimensional reality as a helpless, powerless infant. At a certain point, you begin to identify that tiny body as you, through what has been called "ego-body identification." You come to see yourself as a singular entity, separate from all the other entities you perceive, and you begin to feel fear. As your ego-body identification continues, you also feel profound human feelings. These include feelings of helplessness, powerlessness, loneliness, rage, terror, desperation, and a number of other highly uncomfortable experiences. So here you are, this infinitely magnificent being that now believes you are a tiny, finite being of relative insignificance—and you are extremely *vulnerable*! Those vulnerable feelings inside you, coupled with your perception of your physical limitations, form your core beliefs. The perception of yourself is like a photo album with a series of pictures that make up your overall self-image. As your brain develops, you begin to receive signals that become words that we know as *thoughts*. You experience other, *nicer* feelings as well, of course, such as confidence, serenity, anticipation, hope, et cetera, but since these are not the ones that appear when conflicts arise in your relationship, we will set them aside for now.

Now you have the basic components of your entire belief system concerning who and what you are and what you are capable of, which, at two or three years old, doesn't seem like very much. The equation looks something like this:

Picture + Thought = Idea

Picture + Thought + Feeling = Belief

Ego-Body Identification + Belief = Core Self-Concept

This is merely an illustration intended to point out the function and influence of feelings because the uncomfortable and downright painful feelings that surface in your life are signaling an important opportunity for you to become aware of what you truly are! Blaming your partner for your discomfort is not wrong and is actually *understandable* given the tendency in people to constantly react to outside stimuli. There is, however, another opportunity that people recognize more quickly as they grow in emotional intelligence and awareness—the chance to see your uncomfortable feeling as the power center at the heart of all your beliefs.

There is no such thing as a new feeling. All the discomforts you experience in all of your relationships are feelings you have carried since you were born, possibly even before that, when you were gestating in the womb. They are feelings that come with the body, and in your intimate relationships, your partner is imbued with the special feature of being able to reflect your deepest human feelings. This may be why some marriages bring out murderous rage, devastation, lifelong heartbreak, suicidal depression, and the entire spectrum of human feeling,. Each of these feelings powers a belief about yourself that is 100 percent not true. Your partner is never the cause of your unhappiness, but they can be a powerful support for you to confront your humanness—the belief that you are *only human* being the key part of your self-concept—and give you the chance to *see* the wonderful Truth beyond that illusory facade of humanness.

> *Okay, so my partner does something, and I notice I feel uncomfortable when I see that behavior. So instead of blaming my partner, I feel my feelings, and then . . . what?*

To help you face your human discomforts, it may help you to understand what pain actually is. Because we have a tendency to claim ownership over whatever happens in our bodies, we lose sight of the fact that the pain we experience does not in fact belong to us. You could look at pain as an energy that passes through you and is registered in different parts of your body. Just imagine straightening out a paper clip and sticking it into an electrical socket. Obviously you would experience a jolt of electrical energy entering your body. Does that electricity belong to you? Is it yours? No, it doesn't belong to anyone. Someone else might try the same thing and get the exact same result, and even though they may have a different story regarding how they came to get an electric shock and what it felt like to them, the electrical energy would be identical to that which you experienced.

It's the same thing with human pain. You might contend that you feel you are not good enough because your father always criticized you. Someone else might state that they feel they are not good enough because their father always praised them and they could not live up to their dad's picture of them. Unworthiness is experienced by almost every human being on the planet and may be a major component in the self-concept of each, but it doesn't belong to anyone, and it has nothing to do with one's actual value. But once you make it yours and wrap a history around it, it becomes your personal burden. If unworthiness and abandonment are entwined in your story about your relationship with one of your parents, your partner will be seen to behave in a way very reminiscent of how that parent treated you. How often have these or similar words been screamed at someone's mate throughout history: "You're just like my dad—always putting me down!"?

Okay, so these feelings don't belong to me, and they're just part of the human package. But still, my partner's behavior triggers those feelings in me. It seems to me that I wouldn't have to feel anything bad if my partner didn't make me aware of it!

I know what you mean. Earlier in my life, when discomfort arose, it was a pretty straightforward case of "you hurt me, it's all you fault, you're the villain, and I am an innocent victim of your cruelty." In later stages of my unconscious existence, as much as I tried to be responsible for my own feelings, I could not help but think that, if my wife would just behave in a certain way, I would not have to experience the discomfort that I did. Yes, I would acknowledge to myself that these were my feelings, which I brought into the marriage. Yes, I had carried them around in my subconscious since I was a little boy feeling insignificant and ignored by Mom. Yes, my relationship with my mother influenced the formation of these negative beliefs about myself, and none of that was my wife's fault. *But,* she *still* didn't have to make me dredge up this shit and experience it all again! Somehow, in spite of all my efforts, I still managed to blame my wife for my pain and suffering.

Once I snapped out of my trance and began to understand the meaning of emotional adulthood, I understood that (a) these are not my feelings; (b) I did not carry them around in my subconscious mind because I don't have a subconscious mind; (c) my mother never hurt me; (d) I did not form my beliefs based on what happened to me; and (e) my wife is a perfect companion and a lovely part of my life design. As such, she is part of my life purpose, which at this time seems to be to *see* the Truth more and more clearly. Since beliefs are not the Truth, no matter how positive or spiritual they are, my wife continues to hold up a mirror for me to recognize the lies, stories, and illusions that attempt to block me from *seeing* my essence, or beyond that, the ineffable being that is *Me*.

> *Okay, so once I see that my partner is not the cause of my unhappiness, pain, or suffering, what do I do with the discomfort that arises when my partner says, does, or doesn't do something, and I feel irritated when I witness that?*

I'm glad you asked that; this is where *process* comes in. First of all, I want to state clearly that when I talk about process it's not a spiritual technique, or a healing tool of any kind. I will outline some steps you can follow at first, but you can discard them at some point because it's what the steps represent that matters most. It may also be necessary for you to go through the steps in a space free of distraction at first. Once you understand and connect to the experience, you can do process anytime, anywhere.

Process: Doorway to the Ineffable

I once heard David Schnarch say something that has stuck with me ever since: "When life wants you to grow, it sends you an irritant." This is an appropriate quote to begin outlining the steps of process because when you perceive your partner irritating you, it's a signal that process is available.

Step #1

Catch yourself reacting to the behavior and ask yourself the following: "If I am upset, what must I be experiencing beneath my reaction—abandonment, unworthiness, or heartbreak?" Your intuition will immediately tell you which of these the situation is reflecting for you.

Step #2

Locate the experience. By paying attention to your body, you can locate the sensation, emotion, or feeling. Place your hand over that area of your body. This will support you to keep your attention there.

Step #3

Relax into the experience. Relaxing will draw you deeper into the feeling and carry you toward its center.

Step #4

Recognize the feeling as energy. By calmly paying attention, your awareness will reveal to you that the uncomfortable feeling is neither good nor bad and has all the characteristics of energy. The energy may appear in your mind's eye as a wave, pulsation, or nebulous cloud. It may even have a color and be emitting a sound that only your inner eye can see and inner ear can hear, respectively.

Step #5

Let the process take you where it will. At this point the feeling may simply dissolve, leaving you feeling calm, perhaps joyful. Or perhaps it will guide your awareness to probe deeper, and you may come to a serene, joyful, and loving power that is not vibrating or radiating but seems to be very still. This is what I have come to call *essence*. You may stop doing the process here, or relax even more into the essence, in which case you may disappear, and awareness of *presence* may emerge. Presence is; *You are.* End of story.

> *What's the difference between my essence and what you call "presence"?*

Although essence could be described (albeit inadequately), presence is ineffable; that is, beyond description. Essence is that pure, peaceful, joyful being, expressing itself uniquely through the physical form of your body. It's where all your creative genius, gifts, and talents come from. As profoundly beautiful as essence is, the ineffable presence is way beyond that!

Bliss, peace beyond all understanding, unconditional love, profound appreciation, knowing . . . all these words have been used by those who disappeared and reappeared later to describe the impressions they were left with, but no one seems to be able to describe what it's like when you're there, simply because there is no *you,* no *it,* and no *there* there!

I don't understand.

That's because it can't be described, only experienced. Process is the direct experience. Again, I want to remind you that the steps described are not the experience itself; they are simply supporting you to have that experience.

Because of the importance of this topic, I want to illustrate process in three more ways, with the hope that you can find a description that best suits your character. Whatever method you choose, you begin at the same place—once your partner says, does, or doesn't do something that *seems* to bother or annoy you or make you feel anxious:

1. Notice the irritation, and catch your tendency to react to the outside stimulus.

2. Ask yourself: *What must I be experiencing beneath this irritation—abandonment, unworthiness, or heartbreak?* Listen to intuition's response.

3. Ask yourself: *Where in my body am I holding that uncomfortable experience?* Notice the sensation—tension or whatever—in a certain area of your body. If you have a tendency to be emotionally numb, ask your intuition, *If I were to know its location, where in my body would I be holding that uncomfortable experience?* Trust whatever response comes from your intuition or imagination. Otherwise, just make up an answer.

4. Put your hand over that area of your body, and bring your attention to it. You may see or imagine it as a sort of energy pattern of a particular color, vibrating, pulsating,

or radiating uncomfortably in your body. You may even hear a sound being emitted from it. The feeling may also intensify or morph into a stronger, more profound discomfort.

5. Remind yourself: *This feeling is not real; it's really true peace and joy in disguise.* Continuing to relax into the feeling, let your awareness move deeper inside, into the center of the feeling. You may recognize it as a stillness; it's generally experienced first as flat and lifeless, but eventually there is a pleasant sense of serenity, bliss, or something of that nature.

6. Appreciate the beauty within.

7. You may find yourself ending process here, or you may continue to meditate on this stillness and let process take you further down the rabbit hole, so to speak.

Here's another style of process that may suit you, one that many people new to feelings prefer:

1. Your partner upsets you.

2. Recognize that you are upset, and remind yourself, *If I'm upset, I must be unhappy.*

3. Locate the unhappy feeling in your body, putting your hand over that area of your body if it helps. Experience, sense, or visualize how that unhappy feeling appears in your inner space, noticing its color, pattern, and size.

4. From your heart, remind yourself, *I am the Ineffable Being, creating this feeling in consciousness. It's not real; it's an illusion; it's really true peace and joy in disguise.*

5. *Remind yourself: I welcome that true power back into my awareness. As it returns, I expand in the knowledge of who I really am. I am the Ineffable Being.* Experience, sense, or visualize that power returning to you.

6. Appreciate how realistic the unhappiness seemed to be: *I'm amazed at how real that feeling seemed to be and how completely it fooled me!*

7. Check in to see if there are any more unhappy feelings inside and, if so, do the process again.

You may be drawn to one particular style, experiment with all of them, or take some steps from each and create your own response. As time goes on, you will feel less awkward trying to remember the order of the steps, and you will feel less like you are using a technique of any kind. The flow of process will take over, and you will see that it is actually the unified experience of acceptance, awareness, and appreciation:

1. Accept the discomfort and relax into it.

2. Be aware of the discomfort as an appearance of energy, vibrating, pulsating, or radiating inside you—in your inner space. Be aware of the apparent power source at the center of the energy pattern.

3. Appreciate the beauty of the illusory energy pattern, the power source at its center, and, if you're able to, beyond to the source of it all.

The Three Amigos

These qualities of acceptance, awareness, and appreciation are sort of like three pals that are always seen hanging out with each other. Acceptance seems to be immediately followed by awareness, and soon after, appreciation shows up. When you look at each of these qualities individually, you may realize that they have slightly different meanings than their dictionary definitions.

Acceptance

Acceptance can initially be quite a challenge, because we are often confronted with situations or people's behaviors that we find threatening to our happiness or that we simply don't like. Often confused with tolerance, and even resignation, acceptance is actually a completely peaceful experience of nonreaction. There is no attempt to judge or change what is happening—two tendencies that express your rejection of a situation or person. There is no aggression or defensiveness with acceptance, but simply an acknowledgment of what you are faced with. "This is what is happening" and "It is what it is" are two statements that reflect the preference for acceptance, and you can repeat one of these to yourself when feeling the tendency to reject what is before you. I found that saying, "This is what is happening" has often allowed me to relax and observe whatever is available *behind the scenes* in any situation I am presented with.

When it comes to relationship, one reason you will not accept your partner's behavior or attitude is because it's not fulfilling a need or expectation you have made your partner responsible for. A second reason is that your partner's way of being seems to be making you uncomfortable, perhaps mirroring for you a feeling of unimportance or of *not belonging.* In that case, your partner's behavior or attitude may *seem* to cause you to feel tense and uncomfortable, and you may drop into the defensive stances of anger and blame or accusation. At this point, simply accepting your partner, as is, is not an idea that comes readily to mind. However, it's a step that encourages an ultimately more fulfilling experience within you and between you and your partner. To summarize, you do not consider acceptance because you believe that:

- Your partner's behavior is causing you discomfort and, thus, is wrong and must change.

- Your partner's behavior is not satisfying your needs and, therefore, must change.

- Your partner is breaking a spoken or unspoken agreement and so must change.

The three points above allude to another reason you may have for not accepting your partner's behavior—it interferes with your plans to change him or her.

Acceptance is a magically peaceful state that occurs when you realize your partner's basic character will not change, and that it's not your job to change it anyway! Your partner is who your partner is. Over time, some adjustments in behavior or attitude may occur, but (a) the basic character never changes, (b) no change whatsoever takes place because of your efforts to change your partner, (c) your needs are not your partner's responsibility, and (d) your discomfort is not your partner's fault. Recognizing the truth in those points opens the door for acceptance. In general, accepting your partner tends to take your relationship to a beautifully harmonious level.

It's also important to distinguish between acceptance and resignation. Although resignation can be a step toward acceptance, it is more often motivated by discouragement. When the discouragement is very deep, the resigned partner gives up on the relationship and resorts to a position of grudging compromise or sacrifice.

Awareness

Typically, awareness can seem to be divided in people, where they are witnessing an event while at the same time interpreting its meaning and level of personal importance. In those instances, you might say that their attention is divided between what is happening now, how it's related to the past, and what may come of it in the future. Thus, the mind is racing about in time, while paying some attention to what seems to be happening in the moment. There is no consistency or actual focus in those experiences of awareness and no real sense of being *present* with what is occurring. I might even give it an oxymoronic definition and call it *unconscious awareness*.

Actual awareness is the experience of conscious, impersonal attention or observation. It's much more than the registering of sensory information or experiences that can be had simply by sitting on a bench and watching life's many manifestations. It's an indefinable sense of presence. For example, you could be sitting at your desk, looking at the items on the surface, and you might say that you are aware of the existence and presence of those objects. However, the *awareness* I am referring to is a recognition that reaches beyond the sensory. It's the power of nonvisual observation, where you might say you are observing yourself observing the world. Thus, an awareness exists that *You* are not the body, and *You* are not even in the body. You might experience it as stepping outside of yourself and seeing the situation, and your body as a part of that situation, from every angle possible—simultaneously! Experiencing that pure awareness involves detaching from the personal meanings that you have given to every person, place, and thing in your life, and simply observing them all in neutrality. This means observing the observer as well.

Awareness does not come from the head, though it often *seems* to be registered in the head. This is another belief, equating personal attention with awareness. But since you can be aware of your head, obviously your head is within your awareness. It's like the difference between looking and *seeing*, or hearing and *listening*.

If there is a situation in your relationship that seems to be a cause of suffering for you, you are probably observing it from a personal viewpoint. In those cases, you will often make your partner the cause of your irritation and discomfort. This means you are interpreting what you feel as your personal property, when in fact, those feelings do not belong to you at all. Pain is a universal energy in this holographic reality, but once you make it yours, you get drawn into the drama of protecting yourself, rejecting the pain, blaming your partner for its presence inside you, trying to change or punish your partner, and so on.

But if you step back from, or step *outside*, the situation and observe it from an impersonal perspective, your emotional reaction will dissipate. The simplest way to begin doing this is through the "Loop of Awareness." This tool, designed by Gay and Kathlyn Hendricks, helps you to shift your awareness from what you are observing around you and point it inward to what you are experiencing on a feeling level. You then move your awareness back to the outer situation and then back into the feelings. In this way you remain connected to your partner and your own feelings with growing detachment and avoid drifting into dissociation, while at the same time making emotional reactions and defensiveness less likely to occur.

The following steps illustrate how you can apply the Loop of Awareness while interacting with your partner:

1. Listen to what your partner is saying for a minute or less.

2. For five or ten seconds, turn your attention inward to notice what you are feeling, and how it corresponds to what your partner is expressing. Perhaps you are feeling defensive, angry, sad, or some other feeling or emotion.

3. Bring your attention outward again to what your partner is expressing, for another minute or less.

4. Turn inward and notice what you are experiencing. Each time you turn inward, pay attention more to your vulnerable feelings and less to your defensive reaction.

5. If you speak, do your best to avoid defensive or attack statements and come from the deepest place possible. While talking, notice what you are experiencing inside.

6. When your partner speaks, continue the loop, paying attention to the communication while constantly noticing your inner experience.

At first it may be awkward, but with a little practice, you will experience it as an effortless flow and you will see more and more how your outward perceptions are reflections of your inner experience. You may even begin to be conscious of *You*, the Ineffable Being, engaging in a human experience. *You* are the awareness, within which everything seems to be happening, and what you do and say and what your partner does and says are equal parts of the experience *You* are embracing in awareness.

Appreciation (WOW!)

Appreciation is the wonderful experience of Awe + Love + Gratitude and can only be truly experienced in consciousness, in the moment beyond time. The awe comes when, without the use of any senses, you *see* the ineffable *You* behind and beyond all that occurs in this world. Sometimes this *seeing* is felt or sensed intuitively. By this, I don't mean it is imagined or fabricated by belief. Intuition is seeing through the nonphysical eyes of your essence.

Love is experienced in a nonsensory way and is known to be a power, but not power in terms of what we call energy, and it is in no way a *personal* experience. The love is experienced as unconditional because it needs no conditions, either physical or spiritual, to exist.

Gratitude fills the awareness, but it's not pointed toward anyone or anything. It's a sense of feeling unimaginably lucky to simply exist and be part and parcel of the amazing design of Life.

Love + Awe + Gratitude = Appreciation

That sounds great! Actually it sounds too good to be true.

Only because belief creates an illusion of distance between you and the experience, when in fact appreciation is closer to you than your own body is! It can be experienced at any moment, and only belief blinds you to it.

I just can't imagine feeling appreciation when I'm fighting with my partner or having trouble with one of my children or any time there's a big problem in my life.

Let me outline three ways that appreciation can be experienced. First, during a time of conflict with your partner, you will probably have the tendency to experience anger or irritation, and it may be hard for you to imagine how to bring appreciation into your situation. If you remember that the presence of irritation or anxiety in your life is an opportunity to face a belief and the feeling that is its power source, you can feel the sense of recognition, which is, in many people, a starting point for appreciation. Welcoming the feeling into your awareness and seeing that feeling as pure joy and peace in disguise expands your awareness of what you truly are. As you experience appreciation, which is a natural extension of process, appreciation also goes toward the person who helped you become aware of the irritation or anxiety. When you see this to be true, you will feel a deep appreciation for the support your partner was giving you which helped you see the truth. If you cannot express that appreciation, there may still be more limitations or hurts to face, but you can still *recognize*, and intuitively appreciate, that your partner's behavior is there to help you face the discomfort and the lie (belief) it's connected to.

The second way that appreciation can be invited in does not involve the other steps of process. Process is available whenever you have discomfort in your life; however, sometimes appreciation provides a shortcut. One way you can see this is to recognize that your relationship is inextricably connected to your purpose in life, and so everything your partner says, does, or doesn't do is *perfectly designed* to help you awaken to that purpose. By recognizing this, it becomes possible to appreciate the person who made you angry and how perfectly they did the job which they were designed to do. Even if you can't openly appreciate them, you can begin with a grudging recognition or admiration for how perfectly they *got you*. This practice of appreciation creates the same effect as practicing process when you get upset. You may reach the point where you are constantly awed by how perfectly your partner is designed and for what purpose!

The third opportunity for appreciation can occur during times of harmony in your relationship, where you have the opportunity to spontaneously express appreciation to your partner for what he/she truly is, and how your partner is inspiring you to wake up and grow in awareness of the truth. Be in awe of how perfect your partnership is, how amazingly written your story was that it brought this person into your life. Take a moment to hug your partner, noticing that a body is hugging a body—though the body is not what either of you are—and let the awe of that recognition open you to love and gratitude.

So whether I'm feeling good or bad, I can bring appreciation into my relationship, right?

Exactly! You don't have to like what's happening to appreciate it. Your heart is always experiencing appreciation, and your heart is always present in every situation. Whatever you are dealing with, check into your heart and you will notice that experience is there.

Now let's put the three elements of process together and witness how beautiful and perfect the design is:

1. *Face the situation* and *notice the discomfort* the situation is reflecting for you (abandonment, unworthiness, heartbreak). *Accept* the feeling exactly as you are experiencing it, dropping the whys and the hows, and the story those two words are trying to draw you into. "This is what is happening," and "It is what it is." These two observations help to keep the story out.

2. Notice in detail what you are feeling. Where in your body do you seem to be holding it? Does it seem to appear as a colored vibration, pulsation, or cloud? Be *aware* of the energy at the center of it. Be *aware* of the true power, the creator of that energy, that exists beyond or behind everything you are experiencing. The *you* will disappear, and *You* are the awareness.

3. As acceptance and awareness grow, *appreciation* begins to flow effortlessly. A sense of awe, love, and gratitude grows in awareness and there is *knowing*. It's not a matter of knowing some *thing—things* are for believing. You might say that acceptance, awareness, and appreciation constitute *knowing*.

Even as I write the above words, I am still blown away by the understanding that what first appears as a relationship spat or lovers' quarrel can become the profoundly beautiful experience that masters, saints, and sages have attempted to describe through the ages! What Lao Tzu, Krishna, Vivekananda, Buddha, Krishnamurti, and so many other "spiritually awakened" beings alluded to in their teachings is available to anyone who can catch themselves rejecting what is happening and simply bring their acceptance, awareness, and appreciation to the moment.

What if I'm new to this whole idea of what you are calling "process"? I've been trying to work things through in my relationship, practicing transparent communication, accountability, forgiveness, et cetera, and what I've been calling "process" is the application of various self-soothing or healing techniques.

Techniques have a different purpose, depending on one's level or stage of emotional maturity. Some of the techniques you used may indicate the starting point for exploring your inner space if they encouraged you to feel your feelings. This may not seem like a big deal to you, but in my thirty years as a counselor and workshop leader, I have witnessed a large number of people who do not even know what a feeling actually is, let alone how to bring their awareness to one.

First, let me start by saying that anger is *not* a feeling, nor is sadness or anxiety. You might see a person weeping heavily and assume that they are feeling sad, when in fact, they are not feeling anything—rather, they might be rejecting their feeling of loss through the emotion of sadness and anguish. If they were to actually feel their loss, there may still be tears and sounds of sorrow, but their body language would likely be more quiet and internal. It's common for people to bunch feelings and emotions together, but it may help you to be able to distinguish between the two.

Emotions are typically an attempt to vent or expel one's discomfort. Perhaps you have been to workshops that delve into human feelings and have seen people rolling on the floor and moaning or screaming—maybe even pulling their hair in apparent agony. You may have seen others sitting in their chairs and physically shaking for a length of time as tears rolled down their faces in an apparently endless stream. Someone else might have been raging violently, punching a cushion, beating their hands on the wall, or smashing a chair on the floor.

In Europe and North America, these examples of catharsis

were very popular from the '60s through the '90s, and some seminars still invite those kinds of responses. I used to judge the success of my workshops by how many people broke down into tears every day, until I realized that emotional catharsis was not an essential part of personal, emotional, or spiritual maturation. However, for a number of participants, it was a good first step toward exploring their feelings.

But process is not a healing or therapeutic technique, even though the word has been used in those areas. The process I refer to is not intended to fix, heal, improve, or change you or your relationship. It is available to help you experience True Happiness. Once in that experience, problems, pain, and suffering simply move on.

What's So Bad About Feeling Bad?

As stated earlier, True Happiness is often believed to be a good feeling, and so the majority of individuals spend a great deal of time pursuing good feelings and avoiding bad ones. But since happiness is unconditional, one might say that bad feelings are as much of a gateway to true happiness as good ones are. Now, of course, *unconditional* means there is no actual *way* at all, and the only thing between you and the experience is the *gateless gate* (another quantum thing). So perhaps it would be easier to look at it this way: Bad feelings are not the barrier to happiness that most people believe them to be. Therefore, when so-called bad feelings arise, they can be seen, not as enemies, but rather as messages from consciousness, calling you to open your eyes and *see* the Truth. When we don't divide the world into good and bad or right and wrong, we can accept the dualistic nature of the world and tune into the nondual power that allows it to exist.

So how do I go about simply feeling my feelings?

The following list contains as many different types of human discomfort as I could think of. Not all of them are feelings, but all are human experiences that you are likely to have within the context of your relationship. They are also signals that you are invited to pay attention to, thus taking the opportunity to relax into process. The words in bold print indicate the most primary, maybe even *primal*, human feelings.

Discomforts Chart

Anxious	Sad	Angry	Betrayed
Unworthy	**Lost**	Abandoned	**Lonely**
Heartbroken	**Jealous**	Unloved	**Hopeless**
Unappreciated	**Helpless**	Misunderstood	Useless
Valueless	**Futile**	Inadequate	**Despairing**
Desolate	Bitter	Impatient	Frustrated
Disappointed	Mistreated	Irritated	Guilty
Unimportant	Needy	Annoyed	Insignificant

Discomforts Chart continued on following page

Ashamed	**Desperate**	Embarrassed	Humiliated
Defensive	Suffocated	Doubtful	**Powerless**
Enraged	**Alone**	**Empty**	Uncertain
Terrified	Despondent	**Nothingness**	**Hatred**
Discouraged	Fearful	Distraught	**Meaningless**

You could probably think of a number of discomforts that I haven't mentioned, so please feel free to pencil them into the list! I have not put the experiences in any particular order because discomfort is discomfort. Pain is pain, identified and labeled according to its level of intensity and location in the body (and, of course, the story you want to tell about it). Although falling into utter powerlessness may seem more significant than being in a state of impatience, the response of acceptance, awareness, and appreciation is the same for all of them. I have found, however, that many processes begin with a certain discomfort, such as abandonment, unworthiness, or heartbreaking disappointment and often lead to more intense, *primary* feelings. After all, it was with those primary feelings that our core beliefs were formed.

If you are new to being aware of what you feel, you could photocopy the Discomforts Chart and keep it handy. The next time a conflict or irritation arises between you and your partner, you can simply run your finger down the list until you sense a physical or emotional response to one of the words. You might find yourself connecting to a number of the words, so it's a matter of which one gives you the biggest zap. Then you can ask yourself where in your body this energy is being held, receive your intuitive response, and, with acceptance, awareness, and appreciation, away you go!

Here Comes the Judge!

To briefly recap, few people, if any, can avoid the experience of pain or discomfort over the course of relationship. It is not your partner's fault. Pain occurs according to your life design and the stage of your growth in consciousness and is inextricably tied into your life purpose. None of it occurs randomly or accidentally. Situations and people do not cause pain in us. Rather, the pain occurs and we interpret the situation we are in as the cause of the pain. Actually, all situations are neutral and noncausal, so it's the activation of your own defense mechanism that creates an interpretation of the situation as *wrong* or unfortunate. This interpretation is called *judgment,* and once you engage in it, you solidify your rejection of both the situation and the painful experience.

Judgment is a personal evaluation you give to something, often disguised as a universal evaluation. To say that you like chocolate ice cream is a personal preference, but to say that chocolate ice cream is the best kind of ice cream in the world is to give it a universal value, one that is not actually true.

The basis of judgment is this: Whatever I don't like is bad and wrong, and whatever I like is good and right. Whatever threatens me is bad while whatever comforts me is good. The tendency to judge in this fashion is used in relationships in order to give yourself a power and authority that helps you control your environment. If you don't like your partner's behavior, you can proclaim it as wrong, and then the responsibility is on your partner to make the necessary corrections. In this way, you remain in a safe place of righteousness and superiority, and your partner has to make great effort to atone for his/her wrongness and strive to elevate him/herself to conform to your point of view—which you judge to be the right one. It may help you to consider these points concerning this theme:

- Judgment is a device of your "Defense, Control, Safety, and Manipulation System" (described in detail in Chapter 8).

- Judgment divides everything in your life into good and bad and maintains that separation. However, separation is not true. Therefore, judgment supports what is not true in you and in your life.

- Judging your partner to be wrong usually happens when his/her behavior makes you uncomfortable.

- Judgment reinforces beliefs, and *no* belief is true.

What? What do you mean, "No belief is true"?

Beliefs are replacements for Truth. When you don't *know*, you replace it with a belief, which is a construct of the mind—something that can be thought. But knowing the Truth can only be experienced. You can believe that it's raining outside, which is something you think, but if you go out and feel the rain, then you know, so there is nothing to think about and you've surpassed belief.

Judgment puts beliefs into the good or bad category and

solidifies them there. Since so many of your core beliefs are based on your personal weakness, pain, fear, and need, and because you have judged these aspects of your vulnerability to be wrong, you have judged all your core, so-called negative beliefs to be wrong as well. And if your partner behaves in a way that seems to trigger that vulnerability, then what your partner is doing must be wrong. Consider the following Judgment List.

Judgment List

Wrong (Bad)	Right (Good)
Insecurity	Confidence
Timidity	Assertiveness
Stupidity	Brilliance
Sadness	Cheerfulness
Weakness	Strength
Vulnerability	Invulnerability
Mistakes	Impeccability
Fear	Courage
Emotionalism	Levelheadedness
Need	Independence
Pessimism	Optimism

It seems so easy to fall into the habit of dividing one's humanness into good and bad qualities or traits, compelling one to seek ways to diminish the negative and enhance the positive aspects of one's being. If this is true for you, your personal judgments become the measuring stick for your self-evaluation. Since fulfilling the need for importance is paramount in your life, anything that you judge to be wrong with you becomes a threat to that goal. And if your partner behaves toward you in any way that makes you look or feel that you are wrong or bad, your partner becomes a threat as well. So now you are judging your partner to be right or wrong, good or bad, depending on whether your partner makes you feel right or wrong, good or bad! If your partner pumps up your sense of self-worth, he or she is a good mate, and your relationship is going well. If your sense of importance is not being enhanced, then your partner is engaging in wrong behavior, and the relationship is going poorly. Your assessment of the relationship, then, all depends on (a) how you feel (important or unimportant) and (b) your judgment of how you feel.

Let's look at it another way. Consider the possibility that the purpose of relationship is not concerned in any way with fulfilling your need for importance. Perhaps you think you're in it so that you can feel special, but what if your personal needs, desires, dreams, and expectations have nothing to do with the true purpose of relationship? Maybe relationship is not about your importance, but rather about your *magnificence*! If that is the case, then your personal judgments are not serving your best interests in any way, except to alert you to the presence of a lie that you are holding to be true. Therefore, the compulsive pattern of noticing your partner's behavior; judging it to be wrong; and trying to change your partner can emerge into awareness and be dissolved. What is left then is a whole new opportunity that you can realize by completing the following statements (remember, you can replace the word "partner" with the name of one of your children, parents, siblings, etc.):

- I don't like it when my partner ______________________ . (Describe what your partner does, doesn't do, or says.)

- When my partner behaves that way, I react with ________ ____________________ . (Choose between *annoyance, irritation, anxiety, offense, anger.*)

- If I look underneath my reaction, I notice that I feel ____ __________________ . (Refer to Discomforts Chart on pages 72–73 if you need help identifying the feeling.)

- This feeling is connected to the belief that I am ________ ________________.

Once you have identified the key feeling and belief, put your hand over the area of your body where you seem to be holding that feeling, close your eyes, and let the process carry you through.

Put simply, a judgment always points to a lie that is blocking you from seeing the truth about yourself. Unconscious judgments lead to compulsive, defensive behaviors that are intended to control your environment and manipulate others into changing. When you become conscious of judging yourself or others, you can immediately recognize that you are feeling unhappy. That unhappy feeling is only an illusory appearance, a mere disguise that can be penetrated in order to *see* the truth of who and what *You* are.

That sounds like a huge generalization to me. After all, I've entered many different kinds of relationships in which

I was very clear in my intentions. I formed relationships at work so I could get things done and have a good time doing them. What have my work colleagues got to do with "Truth"? You don't get together with your poker buddies, jogging group, pottery class, ballroom-dancing association, or book club to experience who and what you really are!

When you think about it, so many of the decisions you make concerning what to do, whom to be with, and where to go come from some mysterious source and suddenly appear in your mind—can you really declare that you knew the purpose of each and every decision you seem to have made? What was it that drew you to your friends and your intimate relationships, and what motivates you to maintain these connections? It's easy to say that your need for companionship or the need to feel relevant in the world, or even the need to survive, causes you to form relationships of all levels, but that need is just a physical/emotional sensation in your body. What force directed those sensations toward specific people? What mysterious power caused you to be in a certain place, at a certain time, so that you could encounter the person who was to become your intimate partner?

I once met a woman to whom I was so attracted that I left the city and moved to a small town in Canada so I could live with her. A year later, we broke up, and I was in a lot of pain, so I went to a workshop in Hawaii to "heal myself." In Hawaii, I met a woman. Here are a few points about this story:

- I moved to the small town thinking that I was entering a long-term intimate relationship.

- I went to Hawaii, believing that the breakup was what was driving me there.

- Previous to meeting Su Mei, I had no intention of ever marrying or having children.

- I had never been attracted to members of the Asian races or cultures.

- Su Mei spoke very little English, and I spoke no Mandarin.

- As soon as I met her, I "knew" I was going to marry her.

- Four months later, she left her job, friends, home, and family in Taiwan, and came to live with me in Canada. Although her English improved greatly (to the point where she is now helping to edit my writing), she was far from fluent at the time. But she left her family *and* the man she had originally intended to wed and, knowing hardly anything about me, came to live with me in Canada.

- Ten months after our first encounter, we were married, and the following year we had our first child.

So a man who has no interest in family or marriage, no attraction to women of the Asian races, no financial security, and no ability with languages meets a woman from Taiwan who is almost engaged to another man. She speaks a tiny amount of English, has never been previously attracted to Caucasians, and has no idea how different life in Canada is from life in Taiwan. And the two are married ten months later. How could

I ever claim authorship for such an unlikely story? How could I ever assume to proclaim that I was aware of what I was doing from the very start? Sure, I could say my need for importance propelled me toward this beautiful woman, but that is just the energy that seems to get me off my butt and inspire me to act. As events unfolded, I can say with absolute certainty that I never had a clue as to what was going on.

We often confuse *purpose* with *reason*. We may think we know the reason why a certain situation unfolded, but the purpose of the event lies beyond our limited understanding. If you were to complete the sentence "I got married because __________" with as many reasons and mitigating factors as you and your partner could think of, adding all the opinions of friends, family, and relationship experts, you might come up with a comprehensive explanation for why you entered your relationship. Completing the sentence "I made these friends because _______" may provide a different but similar explanation. But in both cases you would only understand things from a personal viewpoint. The *purpose* of your relationships goes beyond the personal and exists independent of all your reasons and personal understandings. Reasons keep you primarily in what Robert Scheinfeld calls Storyland, whereas purpose takes you into a World Of Wonder—WOW!

With the advantage of hindsight, as well as the perspective that waking from the human trance provided me, I see my serendipitous encounter with my wife—along with everything else that has happened in my life—as an amazing and wonderful living design, over which I had no personal influence. In my heart, I sense that no event in my life has occurred randomly or by accident, and although I see that there were numerous forks in the road, *Christopher* did not choose which road to take at any point. Personally, of course, I would like to say that I have succeeded in my career because I made the right choices and also because of my willingness and determination to keep going. Personally speaking, I *manifested* my relationship with my wife purely by envisioning and choosing it, but that just doesn't feel true to me.

If what I just wrote about purpose is true, what does it say about the mistakes I have made in my life? What does it say about my wife's mistakes, the ones that seemed to have hurt me? And what about the things that I accused her of doing on purpose, believing that she knew full well that they would irritate, hurt, or inconvenience me? When I suggest that *my wife is not the cause of my unhappiness or pain,* I am also implying a much deeper principle, namely *if I am hurt, it is part of a perfect life design, and no person is responsible for either the hurt or the design.*

When I suggested this in workshops, it often got a very unfriendly response from some of the participants, as it sounded like I was letting all the bad guys in the world off the hook. I could quote many respected sources, such as the Ramayana, Mahabharata, the Bible, *A Course in Miracles,* and Buddhist transcripts, to name a few, but that would not assuage their anger. I have always been impressed by the human tendency to hold a certain spiritual principle to be true, but only to a certain extent. Obviously, *love thy neighbor* would not extend to Adolf Hitler or a religious terrorist. When Buddha or Krishna said that the world is an illusion, that doesn't extend to the jerk who just cut you off on the highway. That jerk was an inconsiderate slob who *should know better*! A major lesson in the

Ramayana is about Rama coming to see that his mortal enemy, Ravana, was not such a bad guy after all, even if he did kidnap Rama's wife and try to kill Rama. According to Rama, Ravana was a character in the great cosmic play of life and was simply playing his part.

Don't Take It Personally

I suggest that the hesitation around accepting that your partner is not responsible for your pain or unhappiness is due to the difference between *personal* and *important*. People often get confused regarding these two ways of seeing events, with most of us thinking they are the same thing. When you limit all experiences to the realm of the personal, you will evaluate everything according to how it impacts *you*, the character, personality, egoic being, et cetera, that seems to reside inside that body you see in the bathroom mirror. That identity has mental, emotional, and physical needs, primarily the needs for belonging, importance, safety, and power. How you interpret everything that happens to you depends on whether those needs are being satisfied or denied. But channeling everything you see, hear, smell, and feel through the personal identity, even if that personal identity possesses profound spiritual beliefs, keeps everything contained within the limitations of the little *i*, or *self*.

When you consider what is truly *important*, your intuition guides you beyond those personal walls, and you begin to get glimpses of Truth. I can't prove that my wife, children, parents, siblings, close friends, or anyone else have never been the cause of my unhappiness or pain (especially when my personal memories keep insisting otherwise). However, the more I lean toward emotional adulthood, the more impersonal my perceptions become. Admittedly, this seems to happen in incremental steps (I am only an egg), but I do see enough beyond my personal limitations and boundaries that I no longer take my personal beliefs as gospel.

Understanding the difference between important and personal opens the door to greater possibilities in your relationship. If you don't take it personally when you feel irritated by your partner's behavior, you have the opportunity to see the situation from the perspective of purpose. Accepting *the* discomfort (not *your* discomfort), and bringing impersonal awareness to it allows you to *see* the discomfort as an energy pattern with certain characteristics or qualities. As awareness grows and deepens, stillness comes and the essence of that energy seems to appear. That essence is your essence, the pure and wondrous being or soul that is you in your purest human state. (The first time that essence revealed itself was actually through the mirror of my newborn son. He was no more than ten minutes old when I looked into his eyes and saw looking back at me . . . *no one.*) As awareness deepens even more, all personal influences disappear, and *presence* is. *I AM.*

> I Am
>
> *The joy that never smiles*
>
> *The love that doesn't care*
>
> *The peace never defiled*
>
> *The power that's not there*
>
> *The beauty never painted*

The light that none have seen

The wisdom never tainted

The one who's never been

I AM

To me, it seems there is a simple determination for you to make. Either my words point to a direct experience of the Truth, or they are just part of another philosophy that has no bearing on what people call "the real world." Either your partner can cause you unhappiness and pain, or your partner, and therefore everyone else in the world, cannot be the cause of your unhappiness and pain. If what I propose is pointing toward the Truth, your partner becomes more than simply a companion, lover, friend, and (possibly) mother or father of the children you share. If I am not reflecting the Truth, your partner and you are in a cautious friendship, whereby your happiness is your partner's responsibility.

Reader, be aware: The rest of the book is going to follow the principles of door number one, so if you prefer door number two, you won't find any support from this point onward.

But what about me? Throughout my life, my partners
often told me that I hurt their feelings or pissed them off.

Oh, right! I almost forgot about looking at the second principle from your side! If your partner is never the cause of your unhappiness or pain, what about your responsibility regarding your partner's feelings? When you see that your partner is unhappy, do you believe or feel that you somehow contributed to their state? Do you sometimes engage in a mental dialogue, employing reason and logic to extricate yourself from the blame your partner seems to be casting your way? A simple rule of thumb is that if you feel defensive, or you dissociate from all feelings, when you notice that your partner is unhappy, you typically believe that it's your fault—partially, at least. However, the only real indication that you are responsible is your own feeling of guilt.

> *But I wasn't feeling guilty until my partner started to blame me! Maybe not always in words, but that look of pain on my partner's face seemed to be accusing me of being the cause, so naturally I felt defensive and that I had to prove my innocence!*

You might disagree with this, but really, if you were not feeling guilty, the accusations would come across as simple misunderstandings. It's the guilt that validates your partner's blame, even when you vehemently and desperately insist that you didn't do anything, it wasn't your fault, and your partner misunderstood your behavior.

Let's go back to my suggestion concerning how beliefs are created. Imagine that you are a little child and are experiencing the formulation of a belief. A thought comes into your mind that you are not important. It is accompanied by the image of yourself as a tiny, insignificant body, trying to survive in a land ruled by omnipotent giants. Along with that thought and picture of insignificance comes a feeling of valuelessness. Now you have an energetic belief that is not even a little bit true, but is absolutely convincing in the absence of knowing who and what you are.

Now, what other factor would really solidify belief into an impactful, lifelong self-concept, one that would strongly influence how you would see the world? Isn't guilt the perfect force? I mean, valuelessness is pretty strong in itself, but to further disconnect and isolate you from others, guilt is the ideal reinforcement. Now you feel wrong for being the insignificant person you believe yourself to be.

(If your self-concept were a cake, guilt would be the perfect icing for it. The defenses you build afterward are the sprinkles on the icing, and the candles are your attitudes—those mental compensations, created to liberate yourself from that painful belief and assuage yourself of the guilt. Happy birthday, personal identity!)

There is nothing wrong with you, and you are not the cause of *anyone's* unhappiness. You're just feeling guilty and perceiving your partner's words and behaviors as proof that you did a bad thing—and that you are a bad person. This may sound like a huge rationalization that people use to escape the consequences of their actions, but the proof is in the pudding. Face your guilt and see for yourself. Notice where you are holding it in your body and relax. Simply be with the guilt and notice it. You might immediately notice that the guilt is registered as a sensation in or around your digestive area, maybe your stomach. As you observe it more, you may notice that it vibrates, pulsates, or radiates at a certain unvarying frequency. It is an energy that you have given a name and value to—guilt, a *bad* feeling. Before the name and judgment were attached to it, it was simply an energy pattern that behaved in a certain manner. Lions eat antelope. Volcanic lava burns, disintegrates, or otherwise destroys almost everything in its path. This energy feels like this when registered in this part of the body. From an impersonal perspective, guilt is not guilt.

Once you begin to notice the energy previously known as guilt from a neutral, impersonal perspective, an attunement starts to take place, whereby the power and presence that created this energy can be experienced. It cannot be registered through the senses or by the mind—although it seems to me that it can be intuitively felt—but it certainly can be experienced blissfully, quietly, and free from the illusion of guilt.

Once the guilt is seen for what it really is, you may start to consider that the purpose behind your partner's blaming words and accusatory behavior was to help you notice your guilt, unworthiness, and ultimately, your valuelessness—the energy that helped convince you that you are insignificant and not the ineffable being that *You* truly are.

Before going on to the third principle, I would like to reiterate something about process that is not directly associated with relationships. "Process" is just a word. It is not a series of steps, a technique, or a tool. I use it to refer to the alternative to rejection, judgment, anger, and dissociation/denial when confronted with an uncomfortable situation. I would like to add that process indicates a response of acceptance, awareness, and appreciation when confronted with any kind of discomfort whatsoever. All pain is the same—arthritis, heartbreak, migraines, unworthiness—they're all energy that we have assigned names and judgments to. Discomfort is discomfort—it's all simply a matter of degrees and location in the body. So if you are just acquainting yourself with the principles and are practicing process, remember that it can be applied to any and all pain.

The presence of annoyance, frustration, or anxiety is an indication that an irritant is present and, therefore, as many wise people have stated, "Life wants you to grow." Once you respond to the pain with acceptance, the irritation is no longer needed and will disappear along with the suffering that fades as the acceptance and awareness expand within you. Once process becomes recognized in your life, not only will you see that your partner could never be the cause of your unhappiness, but also that you are not the cause of your partner's. From that point forward, you grow together in the spirit of mutual support.

CHAPTER 3

Sparing the Change

Principle #3: No matter how hard I try, I cannot change my partner.

WHEN IT COMES TO the issue of changing your partner, the majority of people I've met seem to fall into two categories. The first are what I call the Home Improvement people. I have a few acquaintances that have made a career out of buying old, run-down houses, gutting and renovating them, and then reselling the house at a profit so that they could move on to their next fixer-upper. Whenever they enter a house, they envision its potential and immediately begin making notes on what has to go and what can stay. They consider what walls must be demolished and what molding can be stripped and refinished. They check the plumbing and the electrical wiring and all aspects of the structure and foundation in order to decide if the place is worth their time, money, and energy.

In my counseling work, I have had a number of clients who fall into this category. When they fell in love with the one who became their partner, in the backs of their minds they were already making notes about what aspects of the other's behaviors and appearance would have to go and which ones needed to be developed or enhanced. Within very little time, the Home Improvement individual had made a full inspection and compiled a list of all the improvements that would be necessary to make this a comfortable relationship for them to live in.

The second type of client I most often come across is the Don't Ever Change individual. It's almost as if this kind of person wants to marry a living statue. Having fallen in love with the way the person was on their first date, they want them to remain precisely that way, forever. These clients believed the other person was exactly what they needed in order to feel special and happily fulfilled. The future this type envisions includes their partner always being fully supportive and accepting of everything they say and do. Some put their partner on a pedestal, partly out of adoration, but also to keep their partner in one place, unable to stray too far from their original spot. And after all, statues do belong on pedestals, don't they? Other such clients will put *themselves* on a pedestal and expect their partner to remain, staring up at them with eyes full of adoration and praise.

Because the universe seems to love a good joke as much as the next guy (or next universe), it invariably happens that a Home Improvement person will hook up with a Don't Ever Change individual and the two spend their time together in the Change Game. The Home Improvement mate will keep trying to change the other into their vision of a perfect mate, while the Don't Ever Change advocate will vainly attempt to counteract any change (for some change is inevitable) that occurs in their already perfect mate.

Change back or change forward. Either way, the message from both sides is clear: You are not okay the way you are right now, so you must change!

When I was in my *marriage is a lesson in unconditional love* phase of counseling, a woman came to me for help with her marriage, which she said had hit a wall. The following comes from my memory of the dialogue that occurred close to the end of our first session together (with the client's name and a few details changed for reasons of confidentiality). It has the flavor and tempo of the first two or three meetings together. Remember, she approached me for help with her stalled marriage.

"I know I should let go of my expectations of him," she said. "But what else can I do? I just keep feeling so disappointed in him."

"Have you considered accepting him just the way he is?"

"Are you kidding? If I accept him the way he is, then he'll *never* change!"

"Maybe," I said. "But if you really want to learn how to love him, you might have to practice loving him as he is."

She looked at me like I had missed the point somehow.

"But then he'll never change!"

"You've pointed that out already," I said.

"I don't want to love him the way he is," she said. "I want to love him the way he should be. What woman could love a guy that farts in public? I'm not kidding, Christopher. He farts and burps in public. It's so embarrassing!"

"Well, unconditional love means love without con—"

"And he thinks it's *funny!* And he never appreciates me. He never takes me out for supper, or a movie, or even for a walk anymore. He comes home, plays with our kids for a while before supper, finishes eating, and lets out a loud belch. Then he sits and watches TV until he goes to bed. Even after I try to communicate with him and share my feelings, we just end up fighting, and then he goes back to his same old routine."

"What's your purpose in sharing your feelings with him?" I asked.

"So that he'll stop ignoring me. I'm trying to get him to change."

"And how long have you been trying to do that?"

She thought about that for a moment. "Since about a year after we got married."

"And how much has he changed?" I asked.

"Hardly at all. If anything, he's only gotten worse."

"Okay," I said. "So what stops you from accepting him as he is?"

"If I do that he'll *never* change."

"What if he never does change?"

"I don't know," she said. "But I swear to God, if he lets out one more of those disgusting belches at the table, I'm going to kill him."

Let's just say that I quickly became disillusioned with the relationship counseling profession, especially the way I was involved in it. I was an idealistic young man, believing that all you had to do in order to live happily ever after in your intimate relationship was to follow three guidelines:

1. Let go of expectations.

2. Be responsible for, and responsive to, your feelings.

3. Communicate with 100 percent honesty, 100 percent accountability, and 100 percent willingness to be wrong (what I called the 300 Percent Relationship).

The first hurdle I faced in my career concerned point number one. It quickly became apparent that the motivating force in most people's minds when entering an intimate relationship was, in fact, *expectation*. Sure, the client would acknowledge that most expectations come from the need for importance and belonging, but why get intimately involved with another individual if that individual isn't going to make you feel special for the rest of your life? Expectation isn't interfering with one's happiness—it's the way to get that happiness. It's a basic human right for any partner! Pure and simple, I can't be fulfilled unless my partner makes me happy!

The second hurdle came on the heels of the first, when I introduced the idea of being responsible for one's own feelings. First of all, few clients even knew what a feeling was, and those that did saw feelings as a pleasant or unpleasant effect that somebody else would cause. Secondly, why bother feeling uncomfortable? It's human nature to avoid it and look for greater and greater levels of comfort. In the third place, why should I be responsible for what my partner is making me feel?

The third hurdle manifested itself when I looked at the 300 Percent Relationship and calculated my efforts in living up to those ideals. I was embarrassed to have to admit to myself that, even if I added together all three of my own percentages in relation to my own successes, I would not top 100 percent. I was tormented with the thought that I was encouraging clients to live up to an impossible ideal, one that I was failing to even get close to on a daily basis.

The fourth and final hurdle revealed itself to be more like a ten-foot-high brick wall, rather than an obstacle that I could jump over, and it appeared before me about two years before I popped out of my trance. I experienced it as a crisis point, where I had to admit that the relationship principles I tried to implement did not work consistently. That's putting it mildly—they were entirely inconsistent and impossible to live up to, at least for me, my clients, and the other relationship counselors with whom I was acquainted. The basic reason for this, as far as I could tell, was that nobody seemed to understand the true purpose of relationship, and everyone believed, to a certain degree at least, that they needed someone or something outside of themselves to complete them. How could one accept that their partner was incapable of doing so? Surely all one's partner required was a few minor adjustments in order to become the ideal mate. Surely, dear partner, you would be willing to change, *if you really loved me*, wouldn't you?

In the minds of most of the clients I've met, accepting one's partner is akin to resigning in defeat. Acceptance is a great idea and all that—a great idea, but not realistic when you think about all the imperfections in the person you are supposed to be accepting unconditionally. For most of us, we did not sign up for acceptance when we got married. The furthest we might be willing to go would be as part of a compromise, but even then the acceptance would be conditional to our partner fulfilling their half of the deal. Unconditional love and acceptance were just ideals that we agreed to while hiding our *real* intention, which was to get our need for importance met. In order to fulfill that need, our partners had to pull up their socks and start behaving like the ideal mates they were supposed to be.

But then another idea came along. As people reached a certain level of maturity, they came to the conclusion that they must, to paraphrase Gandhi, *be the change they were looking for in their partnership.* In other words, stop waiting for your partner to come around; in order to get what you want, *you* are the one that must change (with the caveat that, once you do, your partner will follow suit—otherwise, get rid of the slacker!). Involved in that personal change were approaches that we called *self-improvement or personal growth or spiritual development or personal accountability or healing* . . . or a plethora of therapies and *paths* that promoted such approaches.

But people don't change all that much, do they? In fact, if you could get your partner to change and become exactly what you want your partner to be, you would be the richest person in the world. Farmers would be flocking to your door, offering you large sums of money and begging you to change the weather in their favor! Deserts would turn green! Barren lands would flourish! Seriously, if you can accomplish the feat of changing your mate, then changing the weather would be child's play for you!

The Naughty Little Demon

If you were the type to believe in the devil, you might come to see that the idea of *change* is the most insidious little demon at the devil's disposal. No one would recognize the plot to make humans suffer because change is always seen as something that should happen in order for things to get *better*. Everyone wants life to get better, don't they? How could attempting to improve yourself or others cause anyone to suffer?

So many of us have attended workshops, counseling, and coaching sessions in the name of self-improvement when what we were *really* seeking is other-improvement. Even when we were attending from the desire to heal ourselves, there was usually the underlying motive of making ourselves capable of improving our life circumstances, our relationships, or our world.

(Sometimes we wanted to change so that we could have the power to make our partners change! In those cases, the participant would be fervently listening to the instructor, and taking notes while thinking to themselves that they couldn't wait to get home and teach this stuff to their partner.)

Well, what's wrong with wanting to change and improve things, Christopher? After all, things can always be better, can't they? What's wrong with wanting things to be better than the way they are?

And there you have it. In those questions lies not a demon, but rather an innocuous and universal belief that negates the benefits of accepting what is, as it is. Generally, when people want improvement, their desire is based on a judgment that what you have now is not good enough, not satisfactory, not fulfilling, or just plain wrong. Judgment exists because *what is* has been rejected, since it did not appear to be satisfying the need for specialness. Out of rejection and judgment come those wonderful ideals that one's partner must live up to in order to get those needs met.

These may appear to be wonderful ideals to strive for, but in none of them is the suggestion that you accept your partner exactly as your partner is. One of the reasons for not accepting (I state with tongue in cheek) may be that the challenging goal of getting your partner to change and live up to your ideals seems far more attainable compared to the impossibility of true acceptance.

Pop Quiz

Let me stop right here and ask you some questions. Please respond from a visceral and not an idealistic level. It will be easy to do this since no one, including your partner, will know what your answers are. If you are not presently in an intimate relationship, refer to one of your previous ones. If you were to evaluate your partner by giving a percentage of satisfaction in each of these areas, what kind of marks would you give them?

Honest and open communicator	%	Expresses feelings	%
Considerate and attentive to you	%	Warmly affectionate	%
Interesting/stimulating company	%	Satisfying lover	%

Now, go over this list again, and grade yourself in relation to your partner.

Honest and open communicator	%	Expresses feelings	%
Considerate and attentive to your partner	%	Warmly affectionate	%
Interesting/stimulating company	%	Satisfying lover	%

And finally, what kind of grade would you give the relationship overall, in terms of your sense of overall satisfaction?

Fulfilling relationship	%

Now comes the real challenge: If you were to close your eyes and envision your partner standing in front of you, what would you experience on a feeling level? Take thirty seconds to do this.

Next, close your eyes and imagine you could look at your partner without any expectation or desire for them to be any different than the way they are right now. That means your partner would not have to change in any way for the rest of your life. Take as long as you want to experiment with this before reading any further.

If you are similar to others, including me, you would have faced some degree of discomfort at the idea of your partner never changing. The first time I did this exercise, about fifteen years ago, I recall the presence of sadness and frustration, but mostly fear. After many years, and more experimentation and exploration, I one day experienced a revelation: Without the need for her to change, I could look into my wife's heart and see the wonder of who she is, free of all judgments and desires. Maybe I had a glimpse of her essence, or maybe it was even beyond that. I don't know, but it was certainly wonderful to have the opportunity to actually *see* my wife instead of all the trappings I had laid upon her, and since that time, both the acceptance and the *seeing* have become more consistent.

As long as the focus of the relationship is on the expectation for your partner to change—that is, improve—you will be unaware of the judgment you are placing on your partner and you will sincerely believe that you are simply trying to have a happier partnership. It's part of human nature to believe that there is a formula for happiness and that once that formula is followed by both parties, to the letter, then eternal happiness will surely be achieved (if only your partner would get with the program!). However, judgment and expectation for change virtually negates the chance for you to see the amazing being you are actually living with. Neither is this *seeing* achieved by *letting go of expectations* or *releasing your judgments* or *healing your relationship with your parents* or, for that matter, enacting any other aphorism or spiritually positive thought you have adopted as a truism. Only acceptance gives you that opportunity.

Before we get to how acceptance grows in intimate relationship (as well as every other aspect of your life), let's have a little more fun with the illusion of change, especially as it pertains to the idea of improvement.

The Self-Improvement Train

Self-improvement (which typically includes *partner improvement*) is another one of those trains that seems to be going somewhere, but ultimately turns out to be going around in a circle. The actual purpose of the train is simply to experience the ride of trying to prove your specialness, but actually, the experience of True Happiness is anywhere off the train. Just get off the train at any point and you will have reached your destination. But as long as you stay on the train, you will be in the hands of your own judgments, traveling through extended replays of your rejection of what is. And what you judge as wrong or insufficient, you will be compelled to improve.

So self-improvement or *personal growth* (which is not *growth* at all) takes you into a realm of unconsciousness where (a) you cannot truly see yourself in the moment, since all improvement is future-oriented, and (b) you constantly compare what you *should* be like with how you judge yourself to be.

Similarly, when you are expecting and attempting improvement in your relationship, your attempts have the dual effect of (1) not seeing your partner in the moment and (2) comparing how you judge your partner to be, with your idea of what he/she should be like. Your need for importance creates an ideal mate, and your judgment creates a false impression of who your mate presently is. When you compare the two images, you are sure to be disappointed in the way you see your partner on a daily basis.

Next, your mind will conjure up ideas about how to mold your partner in order to match your ideal. Some of your methods may include—

- Blaming your partner for your unhappiness, thereby laying the onus for change on them

- Criticizing even the smallest of your partner's irritating habits

- Correcting said habits, even to the point of nitpicking

- Complaining about what your partner is not doing to make you happy

- Communicating feelings "honestly," with the implied message that it is up to your partner to do something about your feelings, even when you are insisting that these feelings are your own responsibility

- Giving advice that's intended to help your partner improve him/herself

- Holding your partner to previously made agreements or promises made ("You said that you would do/stop doing that!" or "Remember, we agreed that we would __________ __________") even when you have not kept all your promises or upheld your side of all agreements

- Doing process while peeking to see if your process is having its desired effect (i.e., is your partner getting better)

- Demanding that your partner be accountable

- Praying for God (Spirit, the Universe, etc.) to intervene on your behalf—for your partner's own good, of course

- Keeping score—reminding your partner of all the things you've done for them compared to how little they've done for you

Unbeknownst to you, there is typically an air of righteousness that accompanies these manipulation attempts, a sense that you are inarguably in the right when striving to get your partner to meet your expectations. After all, you're not trying to harm your partner or turn him/her into a bad person. You're trying to make your partner better, and for some reason you think you know what's best for your mate—or at least that is how your rationalization goes. And where would we be in our relationships without a good supply of rational lies?

No matter how small your expectation seems to be, if you look underneath it, you will see a few dynamics at work:

- The need for importance or specialness, which, as stated in the previous chapter, can never be truly fulfilled

- A rejection of that need because of how vulnerable and unlovable it makes you feel

- A judgment on yourself for being so vulnerable and unlovable

- A compulsion to manipulate your partner into giving you what you need without exposing the need—which would be completely unacceptable

- A judgment on your partner for failing to be the kind of person that can satisfy you

There are probably a lot more dynamics at work, but those five points might give you the idea about what is actually behind this worldwide desire for improvement. And yet, to suggest acceptance often sounds to people like some airy-fairy, do-gooder, wimpy idea that runs counter to the ideology of being a strong, positive-thinking, determined, and dedicated agent of change in the world.

> *But acceptance does sound unrealistic. Like some spiritual ideology that sounds inspiring, but can only be accomplished if you're God! Oh sure, just accept my partner's and my own weakness and vulnerability. Just let everything keep going on this downhill trajectory, while I keep my head in the clouds and pretend everything is just fine—just perfect!—the way it is, and meanwhile nothing changes! Why not just curl up and die right now?*

I am not in any way criticizing the position that human beings have historically taken *against* acceptance and *for* change. It is a great example of how the trance state of forgetting who and what *You* are is so brilliantly surrounded by a support system, designed to make it almost impossible to remember. The human effort that is exerted to change and improve the world seems so noble and inspiring that it obfuscates the judgment and rejection that is at work behind the scenes.

The thing is, once you stop trying to change your partner, you open yourself up to the opportunity to experience *growth*, and there is a world of difference between change (when associated with judgment) and growth in a relationship. Basically, people don't change. They may adjust their behaviors to suit the circumstances in which they find themselves, but they don't essentially change their characters or self-concepts. When your partner doesn't stop nagging you, and your threat to leave is completely credible, your partner might stop that form of behavior. In this way you could say that your partner has changed, but I see that as merely a behavioral adjustment, whereby your partner may continue to mentally nag you, but has altered something in their actions in order to induce you to stay.

If, however, while you were adamantly insisting that your partner should stop nagging you, your partner has an epiphany that nagging is actually a defense/manipulation mechanism that interferes with becoming more mature, the nagging behavior would just gradually fade away, and your partner's behavior would reflect a more emotionally mature way of being. So, in a way, your partner did change, but not from judgment and rejection. The transformation took place the same way a child morphs into a teenager, as part of the natural process of growing up. But you can't force any kind of real change on another, any more than you can force an eight-year-old to change their body into that of a sixteen-year-old. The only difference in this example is that physical growth works on a specific and predictable timetable, whereas emotional growth conforms to a different design. Still, you have no personal power or influence over that design, and expecting your partner to grow or change according to your agenda is actually a reflection of your own emotional immaturity.

> *But wait a minute. Wouldn't my insistence that my partner stop nagging have had some influence on their growth? Wouldn't I have been a catalyst for that growth?*

I suppose it's *possible*. But that's never been my experience. I have never seen any proof that I had anything to do with my wife's or children's growth in emotional maturity. After all, how do you know that it wasn't a matter of you witnessing the mirror effect—that it was actually you taking a step in emotional maturity that allowed you to see your partner in a more mature light? What you witnessed in your partner may have actually been your own emotional adulthood growing in you. Consider this quote attributed to Mark Twain:

> When I was a boy of fourteen, my father
> was so ignorant I could hardly stand to have the old
> man around. But when I got to be twenty-one,
> I was astonished at how much the old man had
> learned in seven years.

But is it also possible that I could actually grow up emotionally and still see my partner remaining unable or unwilling to grow?

Anything is possible. In my experience as a husband and counselor, the typical situations I have seen are that when you take a step in your relationship, your partner takes a step. The timing of these steps may be different, where your partner's step may come two minutes, two days, two weeks, and sometimes even two months later, but it seems that the timing is more connected to your judgment than to your partner's actual growth.

This brings up two extremely important questions: (1) Can your partner say or do anything that has nothing to do with the purpose of your relationship? (2) Is the purpose of your relationship different in any way from the purpose of your life? I would answer both those questions with a resounding *no*.

Another aspect of the compulsion to change yourself or your partner is that the judgment behind the compulsion actually holds your limited perception in place. For instance, if you judge your partner to be kind of coolly distant, and you want them to become more warm and affectionate, most or all of what you see in your partner will be the coolly distant individual. The more you become fixated on your need for warmth and affection, the more your partner will appear to be coolly distant. Pretty soon the desire to change your partner, along with your partner's tendency to resist being changed, creates habitual patterns of behavior in the relationship, acted out compulsively and with little or no conscious awareness.

It reminds me of a time when I was working in a carpentry shop and the boss asked me to cut a piece of plastic that had to be *perfectly* square. I took the proper measurements of the cross angles, carefully clamped down the router guide, and shaved the piece of plastic. After completing the cut, I measured the diagonals and discovered that the plastic was not square. I was quite upset by the result because the material was not cheap, and I could not cut the same piece twice.

I was forced to try again, grabbing another sheet of plastic and performing the same preparations. I checked the measurements between the opposing angles to make sure that they were exactly the same length, clamped down the router guide even more carefully, and nervously ran the tool along the edge of the plastic. I came up with the same result, a sheet that was not a perfect square. Now I was beginning to panic, and even though my colleague tried to calm me down and told me to take my time, I began to work at an even more frantic pace. Well, by the end of the night I had gone through nine sheets of very expensive plastic and not one of them came out square! I realized I had just wasted thousands of dollars of the company's money, and because I was young and insecure—and not all that honest—I decided to try and hide the material. I went about cutting the plastic sheets into smaller squares that I could hide up above me, behind the ceiling tiles. I've cut many different kinds of materials in my life and they invariably came out square. To this day I don't know why I could not get that piece of plastic to come out the way I wanted it. Sometimes, I guess, things are just not meant to be.

When I look back on that time, I am most impressed by the fact that the more compulsively desperate my behavior became, the longer it took to come up with the results I desired. I have seen this same type of behavior in individuals who are trying to change their partner. They don't stop to examine their actions or motivations as their attention to changing that one aspect of their partner becomes a greater and greater fixation. When they complain to others about what's *wrong* with their partner, the so-called fault takes up even more of the discontented mate's thoughts and emotions. It's like seeing a mark on a person's face. The more you see it as something that should not be there, the bigger and more obvious that mark seems to become so that, even while the other person is speaking to you about some very important topic, your mind is distractedly drawn to that facial mark.

Expectations and Preferences

Okay, so now we come to a discussion on expectations and preferences. Let's say it's November, and you and your partner have some vacation time coming up. You want to go to Hawaii, and your partner wants to go to Moscow. When dealing with that issue on the level of preferences, you can calmly discuss each other's point of view and feelings about your stated preferences. Maybe your partner doesn't like hot climates, and you can't stand the cold, and perhaps there are other factors to be considered. An open discussion can bring about a resolution, whereby both preferences can be satisfied.

Now, if you expect your partner to change his/her mind so that you can go to Hawaii, and your partner wants to hold onto his/her preference, then you are likely to wind up in a power struggle, with you being convinced that if your partner really loved you, he/she would let go of his/her preference in order to make you happy. Or maybe you would think that you gave in to your partner last time, and now it's your partner's turn.

Well, what's wrong with each of us taking turns to accommodate the other?

There's nothing wrong with that. There's nothing wrong with whatever way people behave in their relationships. How Your behavior is simply an expression of acceptance or rejection. I've noticed that acceptance creates a sense of flow and ease, while rejection creates torment, struggle, and a kind of jerking motion in people's lives. Let's look at the example of your vacation options: You want to go to warm and sunny Hawaii and your partner wants to go to cold and cloudy

Moscow. Here are the experiences that go with accepting and rejecting your partner's preference.

Accept

- Open and smooth communication

- Recognition and appreciation of the differences between you

- Willingness to consider the benefits of your partner's preference

- Openness to taking separate vacations or exploring other preferences

- Opportunity to experience process if discomfort arises

Reject

- Attempt to manipulate your partner to change

- Resentment toward your partner for not wanting what you want

- Stress of having to be right

- Listening to the other side only to punch holes in your partner's position and rebuke it

- Fighting if discomfort arises

To be perfectly clear, I am not suggesting that one direction is better than the other, or that rejection is the wrong option and acceptance is the right one. Rejection and acceptance are both expressions of our human journey, and the direction we move toward is a reflection of our state of awareness and emotional maturity.

Okay, but what about the slurping or talking with a mouth full of food?

Once again, we come to the issue of preferences and expectations. If your partner's habit is driving you crazy, you can express your preference that your partner curtail that behavior, or you can demand that your partner do so. Of course, you could also notice how much the behavior irritates you and invite process in. In that case, you could mentally invite your partner to keep up the habit in order to support your growth in acceptance, awareness, and appreciation. You know, kind of like, "Sweetheart, it really pisses me off when you slurp your tea. Keep doing it, so I can experience more process!"

You're kidding, right?

Not as much as you might think. It all depends on what experience you want to focus on in your life. If your life direction involves a lot of hard work, disappointment, frustration, and resentment, with the occasional minor victory to keep you going, then rejecting your partner's behavior and trying to change it is the way to accomplish that. If you are in the process of becoming an emotional adult and growing in awareness of what *You* really are, then you will express your preferences without demand or expectation and respond to your irritation with process.

So I should just sit there and listen to the slurping.

I'm not telling you what to do about a specific situation.

What I'm saying is that, in any given situation, you will act from acceptance or rejection.

So I can *ask my partner to stop slurping?*

Sure, or leave the room and go be by yourself. Or ask your partner to go into another room while drinking tea. Do whatever you want. Believe it or not, there is no actual rule book for intimate relationships. You may think there is some kind of code, or set of values, but did these values or this code come from the experience of consciousness or from unconscious authority figures? It seems to me that those codes and values came from people who do not want you to question everything or to think for yourself. But freedom begins with a question because questioning everything, including this very statement and every word in this book, allows you to sense what lies beyond the wall.

What wall?

The wall of beliefs and stories that we think are real and true. Now let's get back to the tea slurping, but this time, reverse the roles. Is there something you do that your mate has a hard time with?

Yes, my partner says I walk too fast when we go for walks. But I feel that I'm not getting enough exercise if I walk more slowly.

Okay, so what happens if this turns into a conflict for you two? Or even a fight? Are you actually going to try and get your partner to change into a fast walker?

Well, no . . . maybe . . . let me think . . .

I'm sure that if this concerned an injured leg, you wouldn't expect your partner to limp faster, would you?

Why not?

Seriously?

I'm just kidding! Of course I wouldn't. I'd adjust to the easiest pace. But there is no leg injury. My partner just wants to walk more slowly, that's all.

So you do in fact have the ability to walk more slowly—you just don't feel like doing so. Look, you could go out for a brisk walk any time you want to, so what if you were to walk more slowly with your partner as a loving gesture? Not out of compromise or sacrifice, but simply to express your caring for your partner. What if you were to give that as a gift? In a way you would be changing because you are a dedicated fast walker and you are walking more slowly, but you're not really changing; you're growing.

Yeah, I could do that. But why doesn't my mate do something like that for me? Why do I have to be the one to change?

This is not about you changing; it's about you growing up. What you might call "real change" only occurs in the natural process of growth. The kind of change most of us have attempted through self-improvement or manipulation of others is typically a surface or appearance adjustment.

But I want my partner to grow with me! I don't want to be the one that's always reading the books or going to the

*workshops—I want to share the growing experience with
my partner!*

Actually, you've been giving a clear example of what I've been calling the *personal* and not the important. You keep focusing on how your partner should behave, and what your partner should do in order to make you feel better. You will not be anything more than temporarily happy (more like relieved) if your partner stops slurping the tea. Soon you'll be busy trying to get your partner to change something else. The Improvement Train—self or other—takes you on an altogether unsatisfying trip. The fact is that, as far as you are concerned, your perception of your partner is determined by your stage of consciousness and emotional maturity. As you grow, so does your perception of your partner. Consider the following:

**Growing = Greater levels of acceptance,
awareness, and appreciation**

**Changing your partner or yourself = Greater levels
of rejection, demand, and manipulation**

Well, of course the first one looks better.

It's actually not a question of better or worse, because those two words reflect judgment. As you grow in consciousness, you will naturally gravitate toward the first. It starts by noticing where your actions, words, and even thoughts seem to be coming from—that is, the need for importance—and continues by questioning whether that need supports Truth or more lies and stories.

Relax.

Notice.

Learn.

Grow.

Know.

It has been a long-held belief that change (improvement, healing, etc.) is the path to happiness. In my experience, happiness is the path to happiness.

CHAPTER 4

Story Time

Principle #4: Relationship problems are just stories.

HAVE YOU EVER STOPPED to consider how much time you spend every day telling yourself stories? Do you ever wonder how many stories you have running at any given time? The second question is especially hard to answer because we don't usually pay conscious attention to the constant dialogues or monologues going on in our heads, but if your brain were a television set, receiving signals from various stations in your mind, imagine how many channels you could access!

Channel Guide (where two channels are listed, one is comedy and the other is tragedy)	
1, 2	Work channels
3, 4	Family channels
5	Health and Fitness channel
6	Food channel
7	Sexual Fantasy channel *(or is this just me?)*
8, 9	Memory channels
10	Embarrassing Moments from the Past channel
11	Money channel
12	Money Fantasy channel
13	Intimate Relationship channel
Etc.	*Well, you get the idea . . .*

To add to the television analogy, when I was growing up, I could visit the house of any of my friends and the television would be on, even if *nobody was watching it*! To this day, I have some friends who have the set on from morning onward, sometimes with the volume way down or muted. It reminds me of my own mind, rambling on with one story or another, depending on which channel I have flicked to with my inner remote, and with the volume at various levels throughout the day. I seem to be constantly telling myself stories, usually stories in which I am the central character.

For many of us, our lives are stories as well, ones which include all the other stories in our heads, along with our interpretations of the events of the day. In your story, you are the protagonist, with a specific character and certain potentials, gifts, and talents, as well as weaknesses and limitations. You, the character, typically encounter situations in which you react according to your personality's predisposition. The reactions and behaviors are predictable and repetitive, and different aspects of the character only emerge when confronted with the unexpected. Your particular character is drawn to certain pleasures and expresses an aversion to what it considers unpleasant. For instance, your character may like action movies but will avoid horror flicks. As long as you are convinced that your character, and the body it's in, is who you really are, you will function according to the strengths and weaknesses of that character, and believe whatever suits the belief system of that character.

(Of course, there will always be that quiet little voice inside, wondering what the purpose of this character, and its story, is.)

Like a long-running television series, your Relationship Story comprises a number of episodes, each with its own subplot that feeds into the larger one. Your Relationship Story in turn parallels and supports the overall plot of your Personal

Life Story. Most of the episodes in your Relationship Story describe these key components:

- Waiting for something to happen

- Facing what happened

- Figuring out why it happened

- Dealing with what happened

- Resolving or concluding what happened

- Waiting for the next thing to happen

Sprinkled throughout the episode are what my friend John Michael calls the "shoulda-coulda-wouldas." These are comments and advice given out by friends, family, your partner, and your own mind, concerning what the situation means and how it ought to be handled. Again, like a television show's episode, various members of your supporting cast enter the scene, recite their dramatic or humorous lines, and then exit. What happens either gets resolved or becomes part of a bigger issue, and thus the Relationship Story continues. Either way, it's all part of your Personal Life Story.

When people are in the unconscious stage of the human journey, the story is everything. The events that occur in their lives are judged to be good or bad depending on how they felt about what happened. They will define everything by and through their stories. If they encounter someone on the street, the event will be a story to share with others. Arguments, gains and losses, births and deaths, even lessons learned are all aspects of the stories people rarely see beyond in the first few stages of the human journey. And the epitaphs on the grave-stones are variations of the last words in a book: "The End."

Problems linger in relationships when the partners interpret what is happening as something that has gone wrong, and then they look for a solution within the boundaries of the problem itself. This ensnares the partners in a story that they try to work through to a satisfactory ending, one that they hope will wrap up with, "And they lived happily ever after." Once you turn your problem into a story in want of a satisfactory conclusion, you have virtually placed yourself in a prison. Figure 4.1 is an adaptation of a model designed by transactional analyst Stephen Karpman, which he titled the Drama Triangle. I altered its definition slightly and included the internal dynamics of its components.

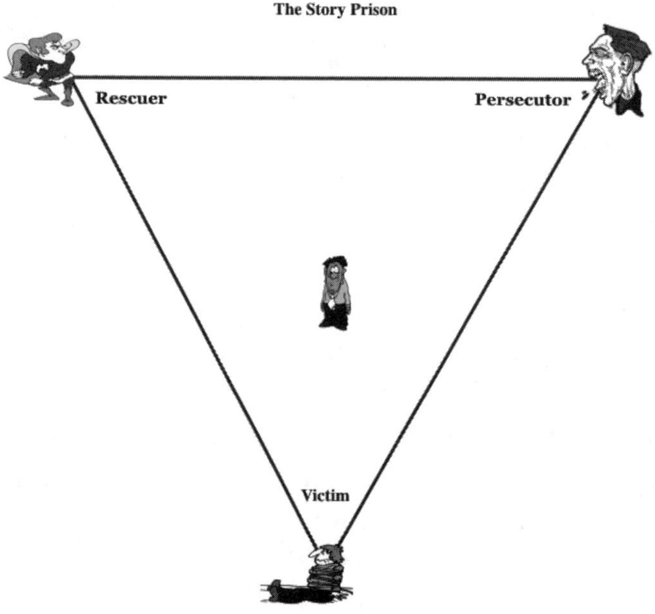

Figure 4.1

Whenever you are confronted with a relationship problem (or any problem with an emotional influence) and you reject the problem, it often appears to be bigger than you. When this occurs, three aspects of your mind become activated and you find yourself trapped in the middle of their dynamic exchange. One aspect is the Victim, which represents your core beliefs. If you remember, earlier I suggested that our core beliefs were formed through our identification with our tiny bodies in childhood and their extreme limitations. Thus, the Victim will initially experience abandonment, and/or unworthiness, and/or heartbreak in the face of the problem. Those experiences are often followed by deeper primary feelings such as powerlessness, helplessness, valuelessness, and so on. Since your important relationships revolve around your need for importance, unworthiness is often a key emotional component in your relationship conflicts and problems. The Victim experience is not a popular one, and if you are like most people, you will try to avoid these Victim feelings, thus shifting your attention toward the other two aspects: the Persecutor and the Rescuer.

The Persecutor is the part of you that angrily looks for the bad guy. It seeks to point out the evil force that caused the problem in the first place and then goes to great lengths to point out everything that is wrong with the antagonist. It will typically point the finger at your partner as the cause of your misery, but can reach further afield and blame some other influential person in your life. However, it can often turn on you as well, attacking your own personal faults and weaknesses as the primary cause. At other times the Persecutor will throw a blanket of blame over everyone involved, including those from your distant past. Sometimes you will see your Persecutor reflected outside yourself. For instance, your partner may be the one expressing criticism, judgment, or blame—or it could be someone else involved in this problematic story. When you perceive someone behaving like the Persecutor, it helps to remember that they are simply reflecting a part of your own mind.

The third mental aspect to be activated is the Rescuer. This is the one you turn to with the hope that you will be extricated from the situation and brought to a state of peace and happiness. The Rescuer further dissociates from feelings, employing instead reason, logic, and analysis to understand why this problem exists and how to solve it. It will constantly give advice and directions about what you should do, think, and say about the situation—not to mention what your partner and everybody else's contribution should be in order to come to a satisfactory resolution. Typically, the resolution involves how you can fulfill your needs for importance and belonging while coming out of the problem looking like the good guy. If the Rescuer cannot find the answer within you, it will point you to a human Rescuer, such as some type of advisor or counselor—or even your partner. Somebody *must* be able to tell you why the problem exists and what you should do to solve it!

And so you have the ingredients for a great human drama, all taking place inside you with manifestations of the Rescuer, Victim, and Persecutor showing up in your external environment as well. Sometimes you will experience being a Victim, while at other times you will resemble the Persecutor or Rescuer, with your partner assuming a complementary role, depending on which one you are playing. As long as you are reacting to the so-called problem through these dynamics, you are serving a sentence in your Story Prison.

Let's look at an example of how a prison story is played out. John (the app designer) and Mary (the real estate agent) have been married for ten years, with the last five years being pretty rocky. The romance is gone. They don't laugh together much anymore, and they have fallen into safe, cautious patterns of interaction with each other. In this scene, John is coming home from the gym after his Saturday afternoon workout. He thinks he is in a good mood, and he just wants a quiet evening, maybe watching a family movie with Mary and the children. Unfortunately, he forgot that on his way home he was supposed to pick up a dozen eggs for the next day's breakfast.

"Did you remember to get the eggs?" Mary asks, as soon as John gets in the door.

"Oops!" John smacks his forehead. "I forgot. Shit!"

Mary rolls her eyes. "John, I asked you to do one thing! How could you forget?"

"No," John smiles, trying to lighten the mood, "you asked me to do *two* things."

"*One* thing! I asked you to go to the market and get eggs."

"See? Go to the market *and* get eggs. Two things. You know I can only remember one thing at a time."

"It's not funny, John. I promised the kids pancakes for tomorrow morning."

"Okay, okay, I'll go out and get them now," John says, discouragement creeping into his tone.

"Never mind, dinner's just about ready. I'll have to go out and get them later. You'll probably get the wrong kind anyway."

"I know what kind to get, the free-range ones. And after the guilt trip you just laid on me, I'll be glad to get out of here!"

"Well, how else do you want me to react?" Mary says, raising her voice. "You're always forgetting what I ask you to do. Or else you keep putting it off and telling me you'll do it later." Cutlery clatters as she starts setting the table.

"And you're always finding things for me to do, and then telling me that I did them wrong!" John shoots back.

"Shh! The children will hear you. We agreed not to expose them to our fights."

"Oh, another thing I'm doing wrong! And I'm not shouting, anyway."

"Well, you sound angry," Mary says.

"I'm not angry! Or at least I wasn't until I saw you."

John senses almost immediately that he has stepped over some dangerous line. Mary stops setting the table and looks at John with a mixture of shock and sadness.

"I didn't realize that I made you so unhappy," she says, her eyes pooling.

"Oh, I didn't mean it like that, Mary. It's just that I was in such a good mood, and then I come home and . . ." His voice trails off.

"Maybe I should leave for a while, and give you time to yourself."

"I'm sorry I said that. I just felt . . . I don't know."

"Not your fault. You were just being honest."

"Come on, Mary, you have to admit things between us have gotten pretty sour."

"Yes, but I thought it was just a stage all married couples go through." A tear rolls down her face.

"Well, five years is a pretty long stage."

"Five years!" Mary's anger returns. "You've been feeling this way for five years? You've been lying to me all this time!"

"No, I wasn't lying," John says, trying to sound reasonable. "Not really." A slight, nervous smile creeps across his face. "I was just . . . being me. You know, avoiding conflict."

"You're just being a wimp, you mean!"

"Hey!" John's defenses are now on full alert.

"What else haven't you been telling me? Are you attracted to someone else? Are you having an affair? Or are you just downloading porn in your office?"

"Right now, I wish I was doing all three!" John snarls.

He puts his jacket back on and, before Mary can say anything else, he slams the door behind him.

While John is driving to the market, he goes over what has just happened, thinking about other comments he *should* have made. He gets more upset as he sees the incident as an example of the problem with their entire relationship. By the time he is purchasing the eggs, he is wondering if their marriage can survive much more of this. And so the story continues in his mind.

Meanwhile, Mary is on the phone talking to her sister, who just happened to call. Mary is relaying the details of their spat and bringing in other examples of how frustrating it is for her to live with John. The sister, Jane, is on the other end, wondering how the two ever got together in the first place, having listened to Mary's complaints for the last ten years. Jane will pass on the story of Mary's latest fight to her husband, as well as other select friends and family the next time she sees them. For the others, the histrionics that go on in the John and Mary Saga are a great source of entertainment and conversation, much like discussing the previous night's sitcom or soap opera. Of course, they also have their own complaints or criticisms about their partners, children, and colleagues, which they will also share for the entertainment of the listeners. Welcome to Storyland!

Let's look again at the event with John and Mary, this time with the view that everything that goes on between them happens within the walls of the Story Prison.

"Did you remember to get the eggs?" Mary asks, as soon as John gets in the door.

"Oops! [Victim]" John smacks his forehead [Persecutor]. "I forgot. Shit!"

Mary rolls her eyes. "John, I asked you to do one thing [Persecutor]! How could you forget?"

"No," John smiles, trying to lighten the mood [Rescuer], "you asked me to do *two* things."

"*One* thing [Persecutor]! I asked you to go to the market and get eggs."

"See? Go to the market *and* get eggs. Two things. You know I can only remember one thing at a time [Rescuer]."

"It's not funny, John [Persecutor]. I promised the kids pancakes for tomorrow morning."

"Okay, okay, I'll go out and get them now [Rescuer]," John says, discouragement creeping into his tone [Victim].

"Never mind, dinner's just about ready [Persecutor]. I'll have to go out and get them later [Victim]. You'll probably get the wrong kind anyway [Persecutor]."

"I know what kind to get, the free-range ones. And after the guilt trip you just laid on me, I'll be glad to get out of here [Persecutor]!"

"Well, how else do you want me to react?" Mary says, raising her voice. "You're always forgetting what I ask you to do [Victim].

Or else you keep putting it off and telling me you'll do it later." Cutlery clatters as she starts setting the table [Persecutor].

"And you're always finding things for me to do, and then telling me that I did them wrong [Victim/Persecutor]!" John shoots back.

"Shh! The children will hear you. We agreed not to expose them to our fights [Rescuer]."

"Oh, another thing I'm doing wrong [Victim]! And I'm not shouting, anyway."

"Well, you sound angry [Persecutor]," Mary says.

"I'm not angry! Or at least I wasn't until I saw you [Victim/Persecutor]."

John senses almost immediately that he has stepped over some dangerous line. Mary stops setting the table and looks at John with a mixture of shock and sadness [Victim].

"I didn't realize that I made you so unhappy [Victim]," she says, her eyes pooling.

"Oh, I didn't mean it like that, Mary [Rescuer]. It's just that I was in such a good mood, and then I come home and . . . " His voice trails off.

"Maybe I should leave for a while, and give you time to yourself [Victim/Rescuer]."

"I'm sorry I said that [Rescuer]. I just felt . . . I don't know [Rescuer/Victim]."

"Not your fault. You were just being honest [Victim]."

"Come on, Mary, you have to admit things between us have gotten pretty sour [Rescuer]."

"Yes, but I thought it was just a stage all married couples go through [Victim/Rescuer]." A tear rolls down her face.

"Well, five years is a pretty long stage [Victim]."

"Five years!" Mary's anger returns. "You've been feeling this way for five years? You've been lying to me all this time [Victim/Persecutor]!"

"No, I wasn't lying," John says, trying to sound reasonable. "Not really." A slight, nervous smile creeps across his face. "I was just . . . being me. You know, avoiding conflict [Rescuer]."

"You're just being a wimp, you mean [Persecutor]!"

"Hey [Victim]!" John's defenses are now on full alert.

"What else haven't you been telling me? Are you attracted to someone else? Are you having an affair? Or are you just downloading porn in your office [Persecutor/Victim]?"

"Right now, I wish I was doing all three [Persecutor/Rescuer]!"

The above dialogue could easily be part of a movie or television script, as it seems the elements of Victim, Persecutor, and Rescuer are employed in most of these forms of entertainment. It's also interesting to me that so many Story Prison stories can be easily written as comedies, even when the characters in the story are obviously experiencing pain, anger, guilt, or shame. If human beings could stop taking their problems personally, we would be able to step back and see how insignificant, and even humorous, many of our so-called crises really are.

Welcome to Storyland

There are internal stories as well, stories that you tell yourself—and others that you live by—without paying too much conscious attention to the narrative. Regarding the ones you tell yourself, these often begin with the posing of the quintessential question: *Why?* Once you ask why, you are inviting your mind to string together a tale designed to provide understanding, a sense of control, and hopefully a doorway out of your present difficulty.

In the outer world, you are likely to get caught up in your personal dramas and feel compelled to perpetuate them until a satisfying conclusion can be reached, only to start another gripping episode soon after the previous one is complete. Sometimes you have two or three stories running at the same time and spend your day flipping from one to the other or juggling them all at once. Anything that happens to you—as well as anything you do about it—if it can be described in words, is story. If there is a challenge or discomfort involved, you will most likely be able to discern the Victim, Persecutor, and Rescuer acting on you, the protagonist. They are story aspects that bridge the inner and outer world. When you perceive these characters acting through *other* people, they are reflecting your inner counterparts.

For instance, if you are confronted with a problem at work, your boss might seem to be upset, yelling at you or a colleague, casting blame about, or threatening some sort of punishment. If you listen to how the boss is expressing him/herself, you will recognize that they are behaving no differently than the Persecutor in your own mind. Maybe one of your parents often took on the Persecutor role with your other parent and behaved in a specific way. Once you grew up and had an intimate relationship of your own, perhaps you were shocked to find yourself acting or speaking in the same prosecutorial way. And maybe you even believe that the way you express your Persecutor is a learned behavior from Mom or Dad. If you think that, you are getting caught in a story, one that is probably not true. You are not acting like that parent; you are acting like the Persecutor that has been influencing every single one of your ancestors—as well as every other human being on the planet. At the end of this chapter, you will see a list of characteristics that apply to the Persecutor's way of being. I challenge you to find one characteristic that is not universal and applies only to you, your parents, or your ancestral line.

Similarly, you may observe your partner behaving in a certain way that reminds you of how one of your parents treated you. Perhaps the nitpicking reminds you of how your mother was always on your case about doing your chores properly, or the constant correcting of what you say seems eerily identical to the way your dad was always correcting you whenever you had a conversation with him. I cannot tell you how many times I have heard clients blurt out statements such as, "After being together for eight years, I realize that I married my mother!" or "When my husband gets angry, he acts just like my father did when he was upset!"

So many people, after they've been in an intimate relationship for a number of years, claim that they sometimes or often feel like they are children again, back home with their parents. Of course, this complaint usually comes out during times of conflict.

There may be some specific ways in which you and your partner express the Victim, Persecutor, or Rescuer, which suit your particular personalities, but that only serves to give your story (i.e., relationship problem) the appearance of being unique.

Well, I disagree with a lot of what you've been saying!

Okay.

I mean, I think my parents had a huge influence on how I turned out, and how I've behaved in my relationships. And I think the same thing goes for my partner.

Okay.

What do you mean, "Okay"? You and I can't both be right about this.

Why not? This is Storyland. I can tell a story about how you are not the victim of your parents' treatment of you, and you can tell one about how you are a direct product of your upbringing. And there are millions of stories between those two messages.

But it's not just a story. It's stuff I actually remember about my childhood.

Memories are stories too. You can make up whatever story you wish in order to explain how you see the events in your life. You can even make up stories about life itself, and your purpose for being here. I know this is going to shock you, but at a certain point, the story *doesn't matter.*

Imagine that you are sitting on a bench that allows you to look at a beautiful sunset. Then you go home and describe it to your partner. You're telling a story about the sunset, and your point in telling your partner is to describe an experience, hoping that he/she can have at least a little bit of that experience too so you could share that beauty together. Would you agree with that?

Sure, but I'd also be telling my partner about it so that I could keep that feeling I had a little longer.

Okay, but what if, instead of getting a sense of the beauty of what you saw, your partner felt envious of you for having that beautiful experience while they were stuck in the house, fixing a leaky toilet and having to watch your two children at the same time? You were out having fun when you could have been home helping your partner out.

> *That would be a real bummer. But that's not why I told my partner about the sunset.*

Exactly! Your story was to support a beautiful experience, and your partner heard that story as a way to prove how inconsiderate you are. Two different meanings to the same story. Stories exist to support a human experience. You could have incorporated that sunset into a million different stories, depending on what kind of experience you wanted to give yourself and the others with whom you shared your tale. How do you think your mate will use that sunset?

> *Probably to let other people know what an inconsiderate jerk I am.*

As well as maybe to get some soothing consolation from others. The story of a sunset enhanced an experience of beauty for you, and in this example it enhanced a Victim experience in your partner. But if you react to your partner's pain by trying to give comfort, you become the Rescuer, and find yourself getting caught up in another story. Or you could get upset back at your partner, become a Persecutor, and blame them for killing the joy you were feeling and wanting to share. Then you have another story. Millions of stories, all with the same basic characters, played out by billions of different actors on this stage we call Planet Earth. And not one of these stories really matters.

Let's say that the story of John and Mary and the eggs is what you might call a Victim story. Now let's say Mary asks John if he remembered to buy the eggs, and John immediately turns around to go out and buy them, while Mary holds dinner for fifteen minutes. What might you call that story?

A very short story, I guess. And a boring one, too.

Boring, meaning the story didn't matter much at all. So what mattered in the first example—the story or the feelings?

But the sunset mattered to me! And my partner getting upset mattered to both of us! You can't say the story doesn't matter at all!

Well, the experiences mattered, but the details were just background. Let me put it this way. Say you've been working late and are really tired, so you decide to get a taxi rather than take the subway or bus home. You hail a cab, get the driver to take you right to your house, pay him, and then get out. Then you walk up to your door and go inside. Now, at what point does the taxi stop being an important part of your life?

As soon as I get out of the cab.

Right! And if you had taken the bus or subway home, the taxi would not be important at all. The function of a story is to point you to a specific experience. Once you are in the experience, the story no longer matters. Furthermore, there are countless stories that could point you to a specific experience, so it really doesn't matter which one you choose. You will get involved in the stories that best reflect your particular character and personality, but the experience it is pointing you to is a universally human experience.

Imagine you broke your arm and, when you got to the doctor, she asked you to give the whole story of how you broke it before she would start actually taking care of your arm. Does she really need to know how and why the injury occurred to respond to your pain?

But back to our sunset story! There are any number of ways that your partner could experience feeling abandoned and unworthy—your watching a sunset while he/she is busy with the toilet and children is just one of the ways that experience could be brought out. So what really matters: the story or the human experience?

> *But wait a minute! My not being home to help my partner cook did cause the feelings of abandonment and unworthiness. If I had been home, those feelings wouldn't have come up, would they?*

Did you create those feelings in your partner?

> *Well . . . my partner might think I did . . . and my guilt tells me I must be the cause. But obviously I didn't. I'm just not that powerful.*

So you see how easily you can use a story to explain why you feel a certain way when in fact the story is pure fiction, which can be used to manipulate others into seeing you a certain way.

*It's not exactly fiction. My partner did feel abandoned
and unworthy, and I was having a good time watching a
sunset while my mate was sweating away at home, so . . .*

But that story only helps you understand what your partner
is feeling, not *why* your partner is feeling that way. It's human
nature to use stories to explain why things happened, but one
of the first lessons I learned as a counselor was this: Whys lead
to lies!

If you're feeling bad, and you ask yourself why you are feeling this way, you immediately activate the three corners of the
Story Prison. The question "Why is this happening to me?" can
initiate the following steps:

- Magnify feelings of being overwhelmed, annoyed, anxious, or even paralyzed with powerlessness [Victim]

- Express the rejection of what you're feeling and angrily
  seek to blame, judge, and criticize someone or something
  (including your own weakness or mistakes) for being the
  imagined cause [Persecutor]

- Send you scrambling up to your rational, logical, analytical mind to explain the who, what, when, where, how,
  and why of your discomfort [Rescuer]

You will compulsively bounce around from corner to corner
but usually keep returning to the Rescuer to figure out how to
fix the problem that is causing you distress. When you try to
implement the solution that the Rescuer provides, and find that
it doesn't work, you might fall back to Victim and Persecutor,

but only temporarily because you are sure that the Rescuer is the key to your freedom from the prison of your problem.

> *What, you mean the Rescuer is not the way out? Not ever?*

Sure, when it comes to mechanical, mathematical, or scientific problems, it appears that the Rescuer can provide guidance and answers—although most breakthroughs in those areas seem to ultimately come from intuition. But this is a book about relationships, so we're talking about feelings. The Rescuer is great at creating elaborate, complex stories around why you feel a certain way—just look at the fields of psychiatry, religion, and psychology—but it doesn't have the capacity to truly understand or effectively respond to problems that involve feelings. The Rescuer wouldn't know what to do with a feeling if one came up and punched it in the nose!

> *So you're saying that we shouldn't have stories, that whenever there's a conflict in our relationships we should just go right to our feelings.*

There you go with the "should" word again. Look, your physical being exists in this world that is full of stories. Everything that happens does so within a narrative framework. But your growth in consciousness and your growth in emotional maturity is not concerned with story.

> So it's okay to have stories; we just have to know when to let go of them.

There's no letting go involved in process. *Letting go* is part of a story we tell ourselves. What I'm saying is that the story can either lead you on a merry little journey around the Story Prison, or it can drop you off at the doorstep of your feelings. At that point, you can turn your attention to what you are feeling and relax into process. Story disappears. The more you grow toward emotional adulthood, the less you will get involved in your stories, except as a form of entertainment and way to connect with others. From a personal viewpoint, stories are real and are what matter most. From a more mature, impersonal perspective, stories don't matter.

So that's what you mean when you write that relationship problems are just stories?

Exactly. Not good or bad, not right or wrong; problems are simply taxis that can take us around and around the Story Prison or drop us at the door to true knowledge. The outline that follows might help clarify what I'm saying.

1. **Situation:** All situations are neutral, neither good nor bad. In fact, any situation or event is part of the overall design of your life and is, therefore, perfect whether you like it or not. As a neutral situation, it doesn't even have to have a reason for being there—it simply is what it is. This is what is happening.

2. **Problem:** The presence of irritation and/or anxiety indicates that uncomfortable feelings are emerging and, being human, you reject your emotions and feelings and project them into the situation. Now the situation is no longer neutral. Now it's a problem that is the actual *cause* of your discomfort, and your emotional entanglement with the situation traps you in the *story.*

3. **Reaction:** Because the problem appears to be a threat to you, you will generally reject it with anger, negative judgment, blame, and criticism, while simultaneously enacting your rational, logical, analytical faculties to understand it and seek a solution to it. Your solutions will involve destroying, fixing, or escaping the problem— or, at worst, seeking a way to cope with it. Your story is now an intense personal drama. (In Relationship Dramas, the solution to the problem is invariably the call for your partner, or sometimes you, to change.)

4. **Meaning:** By now the situation has a completely personal meaning to you over which you have laid personal memories, thus creating a history to support your perception. This makes your story more real, with the frightening possibility that it will remain *permanently* in your life—a never-ending story!

5. **Fork in the road:** At this point, you can halt your compulsive reactions and behaviors and move toward process or simply continue bouncing around the Story Prison. Let's say that you move on to the next step.

6. **Acceptance:** Now you're back to "This is what is happening" and "It is what it is." As best you can, you accept the situation and the uncomfortable feelings that are associated with the meaning you previously gave it. This involves accepting your partner and even going so far as to support them *not* changing, since their particular behavior is affording you the opportunity to face and accept the vulnerability that you have been rejecting.

7. **Facing initial emotions:** You ask yourself what experience(s) lies beneath this problem—abandonment and/or unworthiness and/or heartbreak. Identify the most prominent sensation in your body and relax into it. Your partner is no longer a threat or an adversary.

8. **Awareness:** The more you relax, the deeper your acceptance becomes. Awareness grows. Your awareness reaches past (or through) the initial emotions and you experience the vulnerability of your feeling state. Feeling, although uncomfortable, is quieter and can initially appear as a vast, even endless, abyss. Awareness allows you to see, or sense, feelings in their appearance as energy patterns. You continue to relax and simply notice as your awareness grows. Any thoughts or perceptions of your partner exist to help you see if there are deeper feelings as yet unnoticed. If a sense of resentment or discouragement remains connected to your partner, there is further to go in acceptance and awareness. Personal relationship grows into impersonal love.

9. **Appreciation:** A sense of quiet awe grows as the stillness of pure, peaceful, joyful, loving power grows through awareness. You are filled with the appreciation that *You* are the awareness and that the peace, joy, love, and power of essence are all within *You*. There is also recognition of your partner's essence and appreciation for their service in supporting you to grow in consciousness.

10. **Quantum turn:** The *personal* disappears.

11. Tao, Unconditional Love, True Happiness, the Ineffable, et cetera.

When I was young and still in the caterpillar stage, I could not get past the reaction step. My fear and anger would propel me into compulsively lashing out at the problem and whatever causes I could identify. I would take on whatever survival behavior best suited the situation. My life was a constant example of *fight, flight, freeze,* or *faint.* Therefore, for me, intimate relationships were a source of potential or real torment. The first few weeks of romantic attraction were wonderful, but as soon as I became involved in a so-called committed relationship, I felt the walls of the prison closing in on me. I approached my partner as though I was walking through a minefield, always dreading the next step. I looked at intimate relationship as the prison—when in fact, it was the fear of my discomfort that built the walls.

As I began to grow up, I was more willing to consider that my own feelings were at the root of my problems, but I tended to turn to a professional Rescuer to help me unravel my Victim Story and release everything that was *wrong* with me. Later, my mission to destroy or purge bad feelings turned into a healing mission that involved forgiveness and the development of a relationship with Heaven. Many beautiful moments occurred, and it took me a long time to recognize that I had simply found a celestial place to live in the Rescuer corner. I even hung out my own shingle there and offered my Rescuing services to others as a counselor, workshop leader, and spiritual teacher.

Then, one day, it was time to recognize that I wasn't really a caterpillar—spiritual or otherwise—except in form and belief, and I entered the cocoon of awakening. I turned to the Rescuer and thanked it for the many uplifting experiences through the illusions of healing, spiritual expansion, and self-improvement. Leaving that corner of the prison, I approached my Persecutor and thanked it for impeccably doing its job of reinforcing my beliefs in myself as a limited, powerless human being. Next, I walked over to the Victim and embraced it with acceptance of my vulnerability—my humanness—exactly as it was and is.

Then I walked out of the prison, the place into which I had been born, grew up, got married, and raised a family. The first person I met as I walked through the gateless gate was my wife of eighteen years, and that is when my Love Story began. Even now, as I share this with you, tears of appreciation well up in my eyes. From that day forward, the desire for my wife to change has faded, as my acceptance and appreciation of her has grown.

End of story.

Chapter Appendix

Characteristics of the Story Prison

Rescuer	Persecutor	Victim
Analyzer	Critical	Vulnerable
Rationalizer	Impatient	Fearful
Enabler	Perfectionist	Paralyzed by problem
Pitying	Never satisfied with results	Guilty
Advice giver	Punishing	Unlucky
Smothering—overly helpful	Tormentor	Resentful
Dissociated	Blaming	Insecure
Denies discomfort	Angry	Hurt

Story Prison table continued on following page

Rescuer	Persecutor	Victim
Fixer	Unforgiving	Discouraged
Positive thinker	Abusive	Complainer
Preacher	Judgmental	Self-pitying
Patronizer	Demanding	"I'm treated unfairly!"
Compromiser	Oppressive	Inadequate
Problem "solver"	Threatening	Lost and confused

CHAPTER 5

Love

Principle #5: Specialness is not love.

ABOUT THIRTY YEARS AGO, an old friend of mine and his wife had invited me up to their home outside Calgary for two weeks of cross-country skiing. I was enjoying my time with them immensely when, on the morning of the third day of my visit, he informed me that I had to leave. He would put me up in a hotel nearby, but they needed my room ready for a visit from his mother-in-law. He told me all this with a look of real excitement on his face.

"But Bob," I said, "you can't stand your mother-in-law."

"Yeah, well, now I love her," he said with a smile.

"What? Why? I mean, how did this happen?"

"She just won the State," he said (meaning the Wisconsin State Lottery; it was only second prize, but she won half a million dollars). "Now she's my favorite person in the world, and I'm going to treat her like a queen!"

Another occasion comes to mind. I was in a Hyatt hotel in Tokyo, having dinner with a friend who had just become hugely successful in the stock market. He said that he wanted to help me strike it rich as well. I remember clearly sitting in the restaurant on the top floor and looking out over the city that spanned around us for miles.

"This is where I bring all the friends that I am going to turn into multimillionaires," he said.

"Wow," I said. "Thanks! I love you, man!"

Well, that's not really what I said, but I might have if I could have gotten any words out of my choked-up throat. I had a big mortgage plus a wife and two children to support, and I believed that being a multimillionaire, at that time, would have made my whole life much easier. Although nothing really transpired financially from that meeting, I still remember how I looked at my friend after he said those words.

It's really amazing how need transforms our perceptions of people and situations, and how we seem to behave according to the strength of our needs and desires. It's equally easy for us to confuse need with love when it comes to our obsessive-compulsive need for specialness. I always liked my Japanese friend, but when he sat before me and promised to increase my *specialness stock*, suddenly he was pulled up close to the front of my *specialness queue*. This queue is a configuration of relationships, the order of which is determined by how effectively I felt each relationship was able to satisfy my need for maximum importance. It would look something like this:

Front of the Line (Loves/Likes)

- My partner, children, family members, special friends

- Those who appeared to be more important than me but treated me as though I were just as important

- Those people who appeared to be less important than me and acknowledged my importance

- Those individuals who appeared indifferent toward me— so long as I saw a chance to be important in their eyes somewhere in the future

Back of the Line (Dislikes/Hates)

- Those who appeared to be more important than me and seemed to look down on me

- Those who appeared indifferent toward me, from whom I saw no chance of ever getting appreciation or admiration

- Those who appeared to be less important than me but still treated me as though I were the unimportant one (the *nerve* of those people!)

The people at the front part of the line were people I *loved*, to varying degrees. A little further back were the people I liked— from a lot to a little. Further down the queue were those I disliked, and at the very back were the people I *hated* without reservation.

You might think that "love" and "hate" are words that are too strong for the generalizations I was making—or maybe it's just the word "hate" that seems a bit unnecessary—but I'm trying to illustrate a point about how strong the need for importance is in all human beings. People kill out of jealousy, and what's jealousy, at its root, other than the need to feel special?

If someone is embarrassed in front of a group of people, even a very small group, it can trigger a violent reaction. Embarrassment is really an attack on the other person's *face* or importance, so using the word "hate" is not really that much of an exaggeration. The need to be special is so commonplace that we often overlook its influence. In fact, I bet that it's behind every human interaction that's not involved with actual physical survival.

Back to my former queue—the men and women kept shifting positions according to how I saw myself being treated by them. What were at one time the loves of my life, or best friends, could end up sometime later at the back of the line. Maybe a queue is not an appropriate description for the image I am trying to describe. Perhaps a triangle or pyramid is a more accurate way to describe the configuration of relationships we create based on our need to feel special.

You might call this the Pyramid of Specialness, and you, of course, are poised atop it with the rest of your relationships arranged according to how special you feel—or need to feel—with each. If you were to stop feeling special in your intimate relationship, you might supplant the special position of your partner with that of your children. Someone with whom you're having an affair might ascend rapidly only to plummet again if the affair goes sour. Positions on the pyramid need not even be relationships per se; your work might occupy the position closest to you at the top if that is what makes you feel most special. Whatever you use, you must have someone or something to keep you elevated to that position of most special person. The pyramid must support your perception of yourself as tremendously useful, powerful, irreplaceable, or irresistible.

But with all those shiftings of alignments beneath your feet and the uncertain nature of even long-term relationships—for instance, the constancy of your own children's feelings as they grow up—your foothold atop the pyramid is far from secure. As such, great effort is needed to constantly maintain the illusion that the character you are pretending to be has special significance.

Then one day you wake up and realize your relationships have been under the influence of what Dr. Schnarch calls a "reflected sense of self" and that you have been grading your own value depending on how *you believe* your partner feels about you. You reflect on how your value rises and falls day-to-day, sometimes on an hourly basis. When you realize this, you also recognize that your feeling of specialness in all of your relationships has been based on that same reflected sense of self. And then comes the realization that, even when you recognize your craving for maximum importance, and how much it has tormented you throughout your life, it seems impossible to stop craving that specialness.

Honestly, I'm stunned by the fact that, all my life, I have been pursuing this Holy Grail of experiences—the sense of feeling truly *special*—without ever realizing that it is a futile and endless pursuit. There is no top to your personal pyramid. No matter how much you achieve and acquire, no matter how much reassurance, praise, recognition, and even adoration you receive, it is *never enough.*

Self-Examination Time

Perhaps you can take a moment to confront your desire to feel completely and truly special.

What is it you are trying to experience? In other words, describe what specialness feels like.

What image comes to mind for achieving that supreme specialness?

How would others see you?

How would others treat you?

To some degree of clarity, can you see what your life would be like and how others would interact with you?

Holding that image in your imagination, what does your life look like, day-to-day, year after year? Just let your imagination loose!

Now I have three questions:

1. How many years have you invested in achieving that dream or even a small percentage of it?

2. How much of that dream are you actually experiencing on a consistent basis—how special do you feel that you are on a daily basis?

3. Is specialness real, or is it just a belief?

If you have found, or are finding, that you are tired of chasing mirages in the desert and are more attracted to experiencing the Truth, you come to the very heart of this book: knowing who and what *You* are. *You* are not special, important, or invaluable. These are all human concepts and *You* are not human.

I'm not? I'm confused. And a little insulted, too.

You are having the experience of functioning within the machinery of a human body, but when the body goes, *You* still exist. There is a popular saying that "you are a spiritual being that is having a human experience." I would go further and state that *You* are *the* Spiritual Being that exists beyond time and space, having a human experience within the limits of that time and space. I know, the words don't do justice to the experience. But that's how it is with waking up. You stop chasing after the glamour in life and begin to face the obvious. The obvious may at first appear to be so matter-of-fact and mundane that it's brushed away with a dismissive "of course" or an offhand "yeah, so what?" But let's really look at this: What exactly is your *need* to feel special, and what is it that wants to feel it?

Pop Quiz

If you were to be brutally honest with yourself, how would you answer the following questions in one or two sentences?

- How do you *need* your partner to treat you in order to feel special?

- How do you *need* your partner to treat you when you are feeling unhappy in order to know that you are being taken completely seriously?

- How do you *need* your partner to treat you in front of others?

The following questions are not directly related to your intimate relationship but have a strong influence in your life:

- How did you try to prove your importance to your parents when you were younger?

- How have you tried to prove your importance to your friends throughout your life?

- What do you do to maintain an acceptable appearance in your friendships and in society in general?

- What do you do in your life that is not, in any way, an attempt to satisfy your need for maximum importance and irreplaceable belonging?

Whenever you are serving your need for absolute importance and belonging—or *specialness*—you will interpret situations and events according to whether they can meet those needs. Your relationships will be judged in that light as well: "Can that person make me feel special?" or "Is this person making me feel special?"

The more special you feel, the more love you think you are feeling. But it's not love, because specialness is conditional and ultimately exclusive. You may think that a couple could be seen as equally special in the eyes of others, but within the relationship, there will be competition for who is more special between the two.

If you don't observe your need for specialness with judgment, you could have this wonderful experience in awareness of how that need functions. You begin with the need for maximum importance and irreplaceable belonging and watch how it creates romantic ideals—thoughts and images concerning the so-called perfect mate who could fulfill your need for specialness. These romantic ideals lead to expectations of how that perfect mate should behave in order to make you feel special. When expectations are not met, you launch your *partner improvement project* by expressing your demands, and if these demands are not satisfied, you move to threats and ultimatums.

In any of these steps in your partner improvement project, do you recognize the presence of love, as you experience it, or intuitively understand the word?

The nature of need is to never be satisfied. By becoming more aware of your need for specialness and how it motivates your behaviors, you can see its powerful influence in your important relationships and how its overall purpose seems to be that of confining you and maintaining a limited sense of self. It can begin with a wonderfully expansive sense of romance, filling your mind with images of being treated with adoration, but it will ultimately lead to feelings of disappointment and emptiness.

If you can recognize that your relationships have rarely, if ever, been about love and have instead focused on your need to feel special, you arrive at the following epiphany: that you don't really know love at all, and never will. That's because love is not a thing that you can know with your senses or your mind.

> *So what you're saying is that I've been chasing after a feeling of maximum importance and calling it love, and that I've been evaluating everyone in my life according to*

how special they make me feel? And all this time that I thought I was loving my partner, it was really need I was feeling?

Not always need. Sometimes you were feeling the security of belonging or the expansiveness of importance or the power of thinking you had some control in your life. And there were also times when you felt a genuine affection for your partner or a sense of appreciation and gratitude for what a wonderful person your partner is. But the need always returned, reinforcing the belief that you are not quite good enough and that the best a human can hope for is to die still feeling some degree of specialness. We hope that we will have left the world a better place, made the lives of others richer, done something important, or at least died after having grown into a better person. When you think about it, that sounds like a pretty good way to leave this world.

But you make it sound so, I don't know . . . wrong!

The human experience is great! It's absolutely amazing. What I am saying is that there is more to the human journey than chasing after a need that cannot possibly be fulfilled on more than a fleeting basis or hoping that this temporary sense of maximum importance is the last one you have. I am also saying that you are capable of experiencing that which is not temporary, but eternal. It's directly and immediately available to you because the eternal is what *You* really are.

So I should focus more on my spiritual side rather than my human side?

You really like that word, don't you?

What word?

The Should Tormentor

One of the most significant things I noticed about growing in emotional maturity was how much quieter my mind had become, particularly with regard to the voices of the Persecutor and Rescuer. Suddenly, there was a noticeable lack of *should, must, have to, supposed to,* and their corresponding negatives of *should not, must not,* and so forth. I was truly amazed at the absence, but also amazed when I recognized how tormented I had been by those words throughout my life, for I had given *should* a noble, sometimes divine, designation, calling it my *conscience.* It supposedly guided my decisions and helped me discern between right and wrong. Many people, me included, were quite certain that, without should (or conscience), humanity would consist of greedy, selfish, violent sinners, and the world would fall into complete chaos. However, I discovered that what I like to call the *should tormentor* actually distracted me from listening to the much quieter, intuitive voice of my heart, which is not at all concerned with judgmental words like *greed, selfishness,* or *violence.*

When you bring this understanding into the field of relationships, it challenges one of the most widely held beliefs—that there is a right and wrong way to be in relationship, as well as the belief in a mythical rule book for relationships, a rule book that states, among other things

- Your partner should meet your needs and you should meet your partner's needs.

- There are good relationships and bad relationships. You should always try to be good.

- You should always do your best to make your partner happy.

- You should always be a loyal mate, and you should never cheat on your partner.

- You should forgive mistakes, both your partner's and your own.

- You should admit when you are wrong, and be patient when your partner is wrong.

- You should be willing to communicate calmly and clearly, and listen to your partner's side with an open mind.

- You should always seek a satisfying compromise whenever disagreements arise.

You may have noticed this should-compulsion in others. Sometimes it takes the form of advice ("you should get more rest," "you shouldn't eat so much red meat") or shows up in opinions ("the government should create more jobs for young people") or legitimizes complaints ("it's too hot in here; I can hardly breathe!"). Although the word should is not always used in these examples, it is usually implied. It is recognized as a stress-inducing word, be it *positive stress* or *negative stress*. In either case, however, the intention behind the word seems to most often be concerned with self-improvement or self-preservation.

Often it is believed that self-improvement requires a certain amount of guilt to motivate you. Feel bad about your performance so that you will try harder next time. Feel bad about your body image so you can become more attractive. Feel guilty about your mistakes so that you can atone for them and become a better person.

It seems pretty clear to me that the meaning given to the word should is most often associated with rejection of what is. It also seems clear that, behind these shoulds is a sense of discontent. It's strange how blindly we follow the directions of this one word, believing that its guidance is infallible even when it contradicts itself. One moment it will say, "You've worked really hard. You should sit down and reward yourself with a piece of cake." Ten minutes later, however, it might tell you, "You shouldn't have had that cake. It's too fattening."

> How about this: *"You're just as important as your partner; you should stand up for yourself and for what you want."?*

> Except, of course . . . *"You shouldn't be so selfish; what your partner wants is important too."*

Often, you can have two or more shoulds running at the same time, pointing you in opposing directions and creating a confusing dilemma for yourself:

a. You should tell your partner that you lost a lot of money in that lousy investment.

b. No, it'll only upset them. Keep it to yourself and find a way to get the money back.

a. It's your partner's money too! They have the right to know. You should admit your mistake.

b. Maintaining harmony is more important. You should keep all of this secret.

a. You should be completely honest with your partner.

b. Honesty will only cause problems. You should just find a way to get the money back.

a. You should tell your partner right away.

b. You should delay as long as possible.

a. You should never have made that investment in the first place.

b. You should have consulted with your partner before you did anything!

Hidden in the above commentary are all sorts of statements of blame, regret, complaint, frustration, and judgment, but what is obvious is how tormented the person must feel when subjected to that inner dialogue. Tormented and distracted from the voice of intuition, a voice that consistently gives clear understanding and guidance. Intuition never tells you what you should do because it understands what you are capable of in any given moment and doesn't expect more than that from you. What is constant in your intuition is the state of acceptance. What was constant in the above commentary was the state of rejection—rejection of the fact that money was lost; of what the partner's supposed reaction would be; of the fear, discouragement, and desperation that the individual was feeling.

As individuals grow into emotional adulthood, they recognize the tormentor inside their minds, constantly telling them what they should or shouldn't do or say, and what should or shouldn't be happening. Sometimes they respond to their tormentor with the question, "How do I know what should be happening? How do I *know?*" At other times the tormentor is quieted with the simple recognition that "this is what is happening. It is what it is."

Interlude

Stop for a moment and notice where you are. Look around the space you are in, what time of day it is, what the lighting is like that is coming through the window, and what you are wearing.

Notice if there are any opinions in your mind about what you see.

Notice any opinions regarding how you feel right now.

Consider your life situation:

- State of your finances
- State of your intimate relationship
- State of your friendships
- State of your health

Do you feel a sense of discontent in any of those areas of your life? Can you hear a voice telling you that any of these situations should not exist as they do? If so, is there a corresponding feeling in your body that supports that "should-voice"?

Now think specifically about your intimate relationship. (If you are not presently in one, consider your most recent one.) Consider how you see your mate in your mind. Does your mind tell you that—

- Your partner should be different in any way?

- You should feel differently about your partner?

- You should see your partner differently?

- You should treat your partner better?

If any or all of these are the case, notice the experience inside that supports your should statements. Is it a joyful, peaceful experience? Is it an experience that points you to the truth of what *You* are?

Now, holding an image of your partner in your mind, think about the state of your relationship in general, including how you interact and how you treat each other.

Remind yourself that *this is the way it is.* Not good or bad, but neutral, this is the way your relationship is.

Say it. "This is the way it is."

Pause for a moment to notice what you experience. Then say it again. "This is the way it is."

Stay with this little meditation for a minute or two and then return to this book.

You may have noticed a kind of rebellion going on inside

you—the feeling of rejection growing as your attention turned toward acceptance. Maybe you heard yourself saying something like, "*No!* I want my relationship to be better! I want my partner to be better! I want *me* to be better! All of this is not good enough!"

This is a reasonable reaction, since acceptance of what is actually occurring lacks the drama, glamour, romance, and intensity that is generated by your needs—*especially* your need to feel and be special. Even the torment of should itself seems to have more passion and life to it than the apparent emptiness of accepting what is, exactly as it is. After all, there is nothing special about what is if it is neither good nor bad. But as one grows in acceptance, awareness begins to reveal the wonders that are invisible to a mind busy trying to serve its owner's needs by constantly seeking something better. When all searching ceases, a veil is parted and one witnesses the limitless wonder of simply being, and what opens up before you is the infinite peace that exists beyond all understanding and the unconditional, impersonal power of ineffable love.

> *So I should stop using the word "should" so much? Or I should stop believing what the shoulds are telling me?*

Very funny! No, the shoulds will quiet down by themselves. They may not leave you alone completely—because it's the nature of the personal mind to generate shoulds—but they will have less influence on you and distract you less, as you accept what is happening as it is. When your partner is standing in front of you, life is presenting itself to you. Needs, beliefs, judgments, and shoulds blind you to this. Thus, your perception is very dissatisfying, and you start looking for something else. Something *more*. Something *more* satisfying, something *more* amazing, something *more* . . . more *everything*! But through acceptance, awareness, and appreciation, you come to have a direct experience of life, and there is nothing more fulfilling or amazing than that.

Consider the words of the philosopher Saint Augustine, and notice the emotion and judgment in one line, followed by the unassailable peace of Love's response.

> Experience says, "It is impossible."
> Love says, "It is what it is."

> Pride says, "It is ridiculous."
> Love says, "It is what it is."

> Caution says, "It is careless."
> Love says, "It is what it is."

> Reason says, "It is nonsense."
> Love says, "It is what it is."

> Superstition says, "It is bad luck."
> Love says, "It is what it is."

> Insight says, "It is hopeless."
> Love says, "It is what it is."

I would add:

> Romance says, "It is dull."
> Love says, "It is what it is."

> Need says, "It is empty."

Love says, "It is what it is."

Judgment says, "It is wrong."
Love says, "It is what it is."

If you were to look at all these statements again, which sentence in each of the pairings does your heart tell you is pointing to the Truth?

CHAPTER 6

Always By Your Side

Principle #6: My partner supports me to grow in acceptance, awareness, and appreciation.

IT MAY NOT LOOK LIKE IT SOMETIMES, but every single person in your life is there for only one purpose. Different individuals may be there to support different aspects of that purpose, with some playing more than one role, but when you look at your life from outside the walls of the Story Prison, you see a wonderful supporting cast for the movie of your life, in which you are the star. This can be especially easy to see with your mate and your children; they are always on your side.

So you're saying that my partner and my kids are always on my side.

Yes.

Even when my partner is taking an opposite position when we argue? Even when the kids are doing something I don't want them to do, and they clearly seem not to be see-ing things from my side?

Yes.

How come it doesn't look like that to me when it's hap-pening? Or even afterward?

It will, once you understand your own perceptions and what causes you to see your children and partner the way you do. You mentioned your experience of your partner taking an oppo-site position when you argue. I'm sure you noticed that in all of your conflicts, you and your partner polarize around the issue of contention.

Yeah, my partner's wrong and I'm right—instant polarization!

Good one. Polarization seems to take place in many areas of a relationship. One person may be an introvert and their mate will tend toward extroversion. One might learn by watching, while the other is more of a listener. One might be artistic, while the other can barely draw a stick figure. You may find a clumsy person living with someone who has great poise and balance, an absentminded individual living with a super diligent one, and so on. In general, however, in every relationship I've come across I have noticed polarization regarding two aspects: needs and emotions. When it comes to who needs whom more, cou-ples will polarize around who is going to express their need for the other more, appearing dependent, and who will hide their need and take on the independent role.

Independent	Dependent
Deny needs	Express needs
Appear stronger	Appear weaker
Appear more authoritative	Appear more submissive

Even though the need for importance is equally strong in both individuals, the independent partner will *appear* to need their counterpart less. There are many examples of the independent partner acting aloof and indifferent and avoiding any expression of need or affection until the dependent partner decides they've had enough and leaves the relationship. The independent partner then crashes into paralyzing dependency and desperately tries to win back their lost love. Often, if that lost love does return, so too do the independent and dependent roles, though possibly to a lesser degree than before.

Regarding the area of emotions, you will find the individuals in the relationship coping with their feelings in very different ways, with one tending toward the positive polarity and the other toward the negative.

General Traits of the Positive	General Traits of the Negative
Big picture	Detail-oriented
Deny and suppress discomfort	Obsess about discomfort
Sunny attitude	Cloudy attitude
Overly trusting	Overly suspicious

General Traits table continued on following page

General Traits of the Positive	General Traits of the Negative
Impulsive decision makers	Research before deciding
Want solutions	Want explanations
Problem hiders	Problem identifiers
"Presidents"	"Vice Presidents"
Easy to please	Difficult to please
Optimists	Pessimists (often "realists")
Cheerful	Moody
Expansive	Contractive

(Note: For more detail on these descriptions, turn to the appendix at the end of this chapter on page 198.)

The polarization between the Negative and the Positive becomes much more apparent when conflict arises. Since conflict is rarely seen as an opportunity to grow in acceptance, awareness, and appreciation, the rejection of the conflict accentuates the polarities.

In general, the negative partner in the relationship will often be seen as the harbinger of unhappiness, expressing complaints, criticisms, and focusing largely on what's wrong within the relationship. When the negative partner is not pointing out what is wrong with the other or what's not working in the relationship, they are generally struggling—whether aggressively or passively—with unhappiness or discouragement. Once at work or out with friends, that same negative individual could appear to be a happy-go-lucky sort, with no problems or insecurities whatsoever.

The positive partner, on the other hand, does not acknowledge that there's anything wrong, simply because they don't want to deal with problems. Why drive on a bumpy road when you can cruise along on a smooth highway? And if you *are* in a bumpy relationship, just *pretend* you're on that silky highway or that the bumps are a minor inconvenience, and then you'll be back to cruising smoothly in no time.

In society, the Positive is often looked up to and admired and is even seen as the heroic visionary that brings prosperity and success to the world. It is the positive innovators who saw the value of oil and created all the wonderful products that came from it—the same oil that the negative pundits identify as the cause of global warming, contamination of the water and earth, and air pollution. The negative members of society can also point out that it was the so-called positive members who, when in positions of power, have started every war on the planet, and attempted to exterminate aboriginals on every continent. Positives will assert that it is the Negatives, with their negative thinking, doom-and-gloom attitude, and fault finding, who are the actual cause of all the problems left for Positives to find solutions for. And on and on the debate goes, with each polarity thinking the other is in the wrong.

Agreement and Flow

When you look at a battery, try to imagine how well it would function if there were only one pole, and you will immediately see that it is cooperation between the two poles that creates a sense of harmony and flow. When the positive partner comes up with an idea and consults with the negative partner—who can point out the flaws in the plan—the partnership flows and the company grows. Similarly, in your intimate relationship, you probably experience a harmonious flow when you and your partner are open to each other's points of view, and create a plan of action from the sharing. Agreement comes through such openness, and flow is an expression of that agreement. Where there is no agreement in a relationship, there is no flow, but rather a sort of staggering movement from side to side, with little or no forward motion.

So reaching agreement in all areas is essential to a happy relationship?

I don't know about *that,* but agreement is a necessary component of harmony and flow. Happiness doesn't depend on agreement because happiness doesn't depend on anything. What disagreement can do, however, is help you become aware of whether you are experiencing happiness at the moment. Let's start with how you perceive your partner when you are caught up in a polarity. First, I will show you one more model, which is a combination of the polarities concerning needs and feelings. (A big thanks to Chuck Spezzano for showing me his version of this outline in 1989.)

You may want to take a few minutes to study this model and determine where you spend the most amount of time in your important relationships. Notice also where your partner seems to spend the most time. While studying it, you may notice that you sometimes shift to other quadrants, but there is often one quadrant in which you rarely find yourself. (Note: When referring to the model in regard to your children, you will find that you are almost always on the independent side, although that may change as they grow older.)

Positive Independent	Positive Dependent
Maverick	Dreamer
Super rescuer	Sweet
Tireless	Enthusiastically attentive
Motivator	Inoffensive, whimsical
Producer	Solution suggester
Grandiose (sloppy) thinker	Anxious pleaser, airheaded
Radiant, robust energy	Suffocating/fawning
Blindly inconsiderate	Can be abused
Big-picture person	Puppy dog energy
Negative Independent	**Negative Dependent**
Clear, acute thinker	Warm and caring
Strives for excellence	Quietly observant
Easily angered	Empathetic counselor
Irritable	Pessimistic
Critical and nitpicking	Easily worried
Impatient	Complaining
Perfectionistic	Resigned (assumed inadequacy)
Can be abusive	Never satisfied
	Can be swamped by sadness and anxiety

Notice also how extreme your behavior is in each quadrant, as this determines how close or far you are from the center of the grid. The distance from the center determines the state of emotional maturity you tend to express. For instance, a Negative Independent is rarely, if ever, abusive, unless they are very far from the center and are acting completely unconsciously. One of the indicators of emotional maturity is in one's response to stress. When a stressful situation arises, the less mature individual will move away from the center into a more defensive stance.

Sometimes, you will notice the effects of stress in these polarities when a disagreement or difference of opinion arises in your relationship. Perhaps your partner will complain about your behavior, in that you do not seem to express your affection enough, while you will try to convince your partner of how much you care. In that interaction we see you in the Positive Independent quadrant and your mate in the Negative Dependent polarity. At another time, you may alert your partner to the fact that they are spending a lot more time at work and neglecting their spousal and parental responsibilities, while your partner insists they are making that sacrifice out of love for the family, in which case the roles would be reversed, with you as the Negative Dependent and your partner occupying the Positive Independent quadrant. Let's look at a few more examples.

You, the Positive Dependent, hover around your partner, who is busy with the paperwork concerning family finances. You are asking your partner if they need anything, talking about what happened at work today, and relating something one of your children did at school. Your partner, the Negative

Independent, sighs impatiently from time to time while you chatter away and finally snaps at you that you are distracting them from their work.

You, the Negative Independent, announce that you're fed up with your partner's habit of dominating the conversation when you have company and talking about a lot of nonsensical or uninteresting topics that probably bore your guests. Your partner, the Positive Dependent, apologizes profusely, while looking like a wounded animal, stating in a wheedling tone that they were "only trying to keep our guests entertained and comfortable," and the tone of voice infuriates you even more, causing you to fly into a tirade of criticism, judgment, and blame.

Generally in life, individuals strive to be positive, avoiding discomfort and seeking positive stimulation. This becomes more difficult when you are in an intimate relationship such as that of marriage, parent/child, or family of origin, where one person will gravitate toward a negative position. This is because needs and feelings seem to become more stimulated in those environments. When conflicts arise that are accompanied by strong feelings of irritation or anxiety, you will tend to move deeper into one of the four quadrants while the other person involved in the conflict will seem to move deeper into the opposing one. What is also significant is that the other person will appear to be the exact same distance from the center point as you are. So, if you are being extremely Positive Independent, your partner will appear to be extremely Negative Dependent.

If you were to shift your position, you would witness your partner shifting as well, and likewise if you moved closer to the center point.

What does the center point represent?

That's what I call the Bridge Beyond Your Soul. It represents the Quantum Field, or what has been called by some the Gateless Gate. Others have equated it with the Rabbit Hole from the story *Alice in Wonderland*. Moving toward the center means that you've recognized your irritation as a signal that you are unconsciously rejecting whatever discomfort is emerging and that you're now bringing acceptance, awareness, and appreciation to that discomfort. Process can lead you right to the center and can even cross that bridge to the ineffable. Incidentally, as you relax into process, you will typically observe your partner appearing to change their attitude or behavior in some way.

Do I always have to be the one to go first, in order for my partner to shift? I mean, it seems like my partner has the easy part, and I have to do all the work!

It's not work; it's simply an opportunity to grow up. And it's not a question of *have to*, which is another form of *should*. As you grow up emotionally, you will naturally find yourself moving toward the center—even jumping toward it! You won't do this because you *should* or *have to*, but rather because that is what individuals do when they are growing in consciousness. As this occurs they see their partner differently. A metaphor that is often used is that of the mirror effect. If you move closer to the mirror, your reflection does the same.

To extend that metaphor, how your reflection behaves is completely determined by your behavior. When looking in the mirror, if you raise your right arm and wave your hand from right to left, your reflection will raise its left arm and wave it left to right. It does the same things you do, except in the opposite manner. Remember, this is just a metaphor I'm using to illustrate how this polarity model works. A metaphor to explain a metaphor. The point is that how you see your partner is strictly determined by the position you assume.

So if my partner is angry, it's only because of which quadrant I'm in and how far I am away from the center. If I move to a different spot, my partner will stop being angry?

Or will become angrier, depending on which direction you move. If you try to adjust your behavior in order to *manipulate* your partner into not being angry, you are not moving closer to the center. You may take on the behavior that imitates such a shift, but it won't produce the results you desire. You'll simply be acting unconsciously and out of need and/or fear, and your partner will somehow reflect that need and/or fear in their unconscious behavior.

The purpose of this model is to help you become more conscious. Of course, for some people it might be fun to study it and discuss it with friends and family, but it's not necessary to explore it in great detail. If you begin to recognize that whatever way you see your partner is completely determined by your state of consciousness, this model can help you connect more easily to process. When you notice how you are seeing your partner, you can remember that "the only reason I can be seeing my partner like this is because I am experiencing __________." After that, it is not about trying to change how you see them; it's about paying attention to what you are experiencing. Some examples of how you might do this include:

"I'm seeing my partner as critical and impatient; therefore, I must be up in the Positive Dependent quadrant, feeling nervous and awkward."

"If I'm seeing my partner as someone moody and emotionally swamped, I must be up in Positive Independent land. What feelings am I denying or dissociating from?"

"My partner seems so frustratingly careless and forgetful, and it's driving me up the wall! My Negative Independence must be signaling some kind of deep unhappiness in me."

"I keep thinking that my partner is distant and inconsiderate of how I feel, but it must be me, drowning in Negative Dependency, getting lost in my emotional story and not paying attention to the really important feelings inside me."

I hope you realize that nobody in the world talks like that—not even in bad movies.

But you get the point, right? Every perception you have—not only of your partner, but of everyone and everything in the world—is determined by you and what you are experiencing. You could easily see this if you looked in the mirror more and asked, "How am I seeing myself today?"

People do not see themselves in the exact same way all the time. Sometimes you will look in the mirror and like what you see; other times, not so much, even though your physical appearance does not change that significantly from one day to the next.

Similarly, even though your partner does not change all that much day-to-day, *how* you see your partner changes radically according to what you are experiencing inside and whether you are aware or unaware of it—accepting or rejecting it.

In previous chapters, I stated that your partner can act as an irritant to help you become aware of a discomfort inside you. Actually, on those occasions when they seem to be irritating you, your partner is not in fact the irritant but merely a reflection of the annoyance or anxiety within you.

There is a big difference between the roles that your partner will play in the caterpillar, or unconscious, stage and the roles of the cocoon, or awakening, stage. Compare the following:

When you are relatively or completely unconscious, your partner can be perceived as

- A threat, or cause of pain

- A teacher of beliefs, or Rescuer

- A conditional or cautious friend

As you expand in consciousness and grow toward emotional adulthood, your partner can be perceived as

- A mirror, or signaler of process

- An inspirer, or teacher of Truth

- A playmate or companion

As a matter of fact, the above descriptions apply to every single person you encounter in your life. The *threat* is an enemy or potential enemy. It can be someone who hurt you in the past, who is hurting you now, or who could potentially hurt you in the future if given the opportunity. The *teacher* is someone who gives you information and guidance and helps you function more capably in the world or who helps you keep searching for that which can never be found. The *conditional friend* is the best you can do concerning relationships in the unconscious stage. It may be a confidante, intimate partner, family member, or someone with whom you share a common interest. Whether you call that person your soul mate, best friend, good buddy, or casual acquaintance, there is always a certain degree of caution between you, fueled by the belief that this person is capable of hurting, embarrassing, or betraying you. Those closest to you can assume any of the three roles, depending on the circumstances in your life. A husband or wife can switch from being a teacher to a cautious friend and then to a threat all in one day.

Upon entering the cocoon, you recognize that no belief is true, that no one can make you happy or unhappy, and that every aspect of life exists to help you remember what *You* really are. At this point, your relationships, from intimate to distant, seem to undergo a transformation. They are the same people, with the same characteristics they've always had, but because of the metamorphosis you are undergoing, you begin to see them differently. Since no one can hurt you, the threat is seen simply as a reflection, mirroring for you some human discomfort that is fueling a belief, which in turn is blinding you to the truth.

In the caterpillar stage, the function of the teacher was to help you maintain your beliefs (even if you regarded that teacher as an enlightened or spiritually advanced being). In the cocoon, the teacher becomes someone who inspires and supports you to see *through* beliefs and experience what awaits you beyond. You are often surprised by the depth of your partner's wisdom and clarity, even when what they are telling you is something you've heard many times before. This is because, in the past, you only *heard,* whereas now you can *listen.*

Lastly, a cautious friendship will seem to morph into another kind of relationship—that of a playmate. There can be more lightness because your need for importance becomes less of a burden and you can simply enjoy the wonder of existence in this virtual reality we call the world. People, even the stranger passing by you on the sidewalk, or sharing a step on an escalator, become a beautiful part of your life, even if it's only for a brief moment. Life becomes more akin to a play or movie and you experience interactions with others as actors speaking their lines according to the roles they play. There is a wonderful sense of serendipity with each encounter when you see them as playmates in this amazing amusement park or playground.

In your intimate relationship, your partner will move from one role to the next depending on what human/spiritual experience the moment is offering you, but you won't be able to forget for any length of time that your partner exists as someone who is supporting you completely to remember what you are and why you are here.

> *Is it possible for me to be in the cocoon and my partner to remain in the caterpillar stage?*

Anything is possible, and whether that happens is not really important. What matters is how you are perceiving the people and events in your life.

Yeah, but if I wake up or grow up or whatever, then I won't be able to share what I'm experiencing. Or if I do, my partner won't understand what I'm saying or feeling.

Then that is what's most important for you to experience. If it makes you uncomfortable, you can relax into process. If not, you can simply appreciate your partner for being who they are. Either way, you can't lose. Your appreciation for your partner will grow, regardless of the stage you *think* they're in, and your partner will continue to be your mirror, teacher, and/ or playmate.

Merrily, Merrily, Merrily, Merrily, Life Is but a Dream

Let's look at your situation, using a few different analogies. First, we'll begin with the idea of seeing your life as a dream. Let's say that you're asleep in bed one night, and you dream that you and your partner are sitting at your kitchen table when suddenly an attractive stranger walks in and starts kissing your partner. What do you think you would feel if that happened?

I think I'd be really angry. And if I were to look deeper . . . heartbroken, maybe, and also pretty worthless or insignificant.

Okay, so now I have three questions. First, would the *you* in the dream feel that or the *you* sleeping in bed?

Well, both, I guess.

So that *you* in the dream has real feelings. If you were to die in the dream, you'd really die in bed, too?

No, of course not. I've had a lot of dreams where I died, and I'm still here! So I guess, when I think about it, only the me that's in bed asleep is feeling the hurt, but I think I'm in the kitchen, feeling it there.

Okay, so now my second question: When you wake up, would you turn to your partner and accuse them of betraying you?

Actually, I did do that once, when I dreamed that my partner was having an affair. I was mad for two days.

And then what?

Well, I realized I was being ridiculous and my partner and I ended up having a good laugh about it.

Which brings me to my third question: Who was it that made your partner start making out with an attractive stranger?

Nobody—it was just a dream!

Ah, but who is doing the dreaming?

Okay, I get what you're saying. I made the whole thing happen.

Including the interpretation you gave it, that your partner was betraying you. You could have dreamed a different interpretation, or you could have dreamed of an attractive stranger coming in and kissing you in front of your partner. You're the creator of all that occurred. Now imagine that this world is part of a dream, and you, meaning *You,* are not here. You're lying in a bed in Nowhere Land, dreaming this whole thing up. Everything that happens is all part of *Your* dream. Can your partner say or do anything unless *You* dream it that way?

No, I guess not.

So maybe you could look at your relationship that way, like everything your partner says or does is purely because *You* dreamed it that way.

But what would be the purpose of that? Why would I dream my partner to be that specific way?

That reminds me of a story I heard. A woman is dreaming that she's walking on a deserted street, when suddenly she sees a scary monster running toward her. So she starts running away, but no matter what she does, she can't seem to get away from it. She runs into a building and locks the door, turns, and sees the monster right behind her. So she jumps out the window and keeps running. She keeps trying to elude it, but all her efforts are futile. Then she runs down an alley and it turns out to be a dead end. She reaches a brick wall and, realizing there's no escape, turns to face the monster and screams, "What the fuck do you want from me?" To which the monster replies, "Don't ask me, lady. It's your dream!"

Good story, but how does that answer my question: What's the purpose of me dreaming my partner to be exactly the way my partner is?

I don't know, what's the purpose of any dream? It begins, you experience it, and then it ends. The only purpose I can see to this dream of being human is to fully experience every aspect of it. But why I introduced this metaphor was because maybe it could help you with your interactions in your relationship. When your partner behaves a certain way that you dislike, you can remind yourself that it's the only way your partner *could* have behaved in that moment because that is the way *You* dreamed it. If that statement feels *true* to you in your heart, then it can inspire you to see more clearly. But if it makes no sense to you, or doesn't feel right, ignore the metaphor.

The Play's the Thing

Another way you could view your life is through the metaphor of the play. If you've ever watched a live performance, you will recognize how strictly the actors recite their lines. The play could be on Broadway for years, and every night the actors would repeat the same lines because they behave according to the script. *The Lion King* would not be *The Lion King* if the actors shouted out any line they felt like shouting, or sang different songs from the ones they were hired to sing. *The Lion King* had a specific message and meaning, which the creator of the play wanted to convey, and so the script had to be followed in order to fulfill the creator's purpose.

Now let's say that you have a specific purpose and meaning to your life, so the creator—*You*—designs a script that perfectly fulfills that purpose. Every aspect, event, and person then follows that script to the letter. Nothing is random and there are no accidents; everything follows the design perfectly. That means that your partner is not to blame for any hurt, annoyance, or anxiety you experience because every actor in the play you know as your life is simply following the script. Remembering this just makes it easier for you to disengage from any emotional reaction or power struggle and to turn inside to what awaits you there.

How do I know you're telling the truth? Or that the dream or play metaphor has any truth to it at all?

The metaphors are not the Truth; they're simply pointing you toward the Truth. Whether in fact they are actually doing that or whether I am telling the Truth, well, either I am or I'm not. Your heart can recognize which it is. Recognizing that my wife and children were acting according to a script helped me at a certain time in my life to grow in acceptance and turned me toward process more quickly and directly. At another time in my life, it was helpful to recognize that my wife and children—and other people as well—could only appear to be acting a certain way because of the quadrant I was in. Neither of these approaches, or any of the other ones mentioned in this book, are *the Truth*. In the past, some of them were supportive of a direct experience of Truth, and some still are from time to time. But not one single word in this book is *the Truth*.

Life as a Video Game

While we are on the subject of helpful metaphors, another one that comes to mind concerns video games, specifically role-playing ones, where you choose a character and send it on some sort of adventure. It's easy to get so involved that you're actually feeling fear, discouragement, excitement, and even jealousy or envy toward other characters and a wide spectrum of other feelings and emotions. Whether you end the game in victory or defeat, the characters all disappear from the screen and you come away having had an experience. That is why you play the game—to have an experience. You might also notice that every character in the game is defined by its strengths and weaknesses. That is pretty much what a character is, something with strengths, weaknesses, potential, and limitation. Throughout the game, the character remains true to its characteristics because that is how the game is designed. In your Relationship Game, which is part of your Human Game, your behaviors are determined by your character, and that character is designed to have certain experiences. A major experience comes from believing that all you are *is* that character, which, in the human journey, can be followed by another experience of realizing you are *not* that character.

There are a seemingly infinite number of experiences in this 3-D (or 5-D if you include time and thought—or possibly more) virtual reality role-playing game, and every character begins by believing that they, and the game, are real. If you think the character riding around in your body is real, then you will think that your partner's character is real and operates independently from you. This is true as long as you believe you are the personality. When you enter the cocoon, *vision* begins to expand, and you see beyond the beliefs, leading you to the intuitive insight that every character's behavior is interconnected with those of all the other characters, and there is a sense of inevitability in all the interactions that take place. Of *course* your partner is saying that, or doing that, and at this specific time and place! And the purpose of those words or that behavior is to act as your mirror, teacher, or playmate, affording you the opportunity to experience acceptance, awareness, and appreciation—allowing you to *know*!

It's just so perfect! When you truly see this, all the metaphors merge—the dream, play, computer game—and there it is! The wonderful, limitless, meaningless experience of life. You are that life!

> *Wow! That's really amazing—if it's all true. But I still don't get why. Why is life like that? I mean, I enjoy my life and I appreciate my partner and the kids. I really love them, but I don't understand why we have to live like caterpillars, then enter the cocoon, and come out as butterflies, if* we even make it out of the cocoon! Or even into it! I just can't stop wondering why I'm here . . .*

As I mentioned earlier, whys lead to lies. The word *why* is designed to point us to our limited intellects in order to try to understand the limitless, and it's a futile undertaking. But although we may not be able to understand intellectually, it is possible to experience the design in consciousness. As I'm writing these words, I am sitting on a sofa in a vacation suite we have rented in Whistler, British Columbia. My wife is sitting at the kitchen table, working on her computer. My eyes are staring at the fireplace, and there is an awareness of her nearby, but there is a sense that *I* am not here. These bodies exist in the outside world, in what Robert Scheinfeld calls Storyland, but *I* am not this body. *I* am not *in* this body either, although it does seem as though *I* am looking out through its eyes.

But awareness of what these eyes see is not inside this body, and *I* am the awareness. The awareness is not in this room, in the town of Whistler, or even in this world, this Storyland. *I* am not here. I could go on to describe this amazing experience I am having, but the point I am attempting to make is that this experience is not coming because I asked *why*. The Why Train is another wonderful human ride that goes around in circles, so I will leave you to pursue the question in other books of philosophy, psychology, or spirituality, and we can continue to explore the topic of relationship—its design and purpose.

If you could entertain the possibility that what I have written points toward the experience of truth, you might also consider that relationship has been designed not by people, but by an amazing intelligence, wisdom, and creativity that is far beyond human comprehension. And the purpose of relationship is to help you become aware of that magnificent power (which, by the way, *You* are). This purpose is realized as you grow in acceptance, awareness, and appreciation, so let's look at how these three qualities grow in us.

The Three Amigos Ride Again

As I wrote in a previous chapter, acceptance often proves to be extremely challenging for people, but that is usually because it is associated with the personal feelings of ultimate discouragement or resignation. Resignation reflects the belief that we have lost any chance for real happiness, success, fulfillment, or abundance because we are just not important (or not important enough). When acceptance is associated with resignation, it's easy to understand why people automatically reject the idea of acceptance as anything close to a wonderful experience, but that is because acceptance has been given a personal interpretation. Acceptance is not personal. It is, however, joyfully liberating! So how does one move from the personal and discouraging feeling of resignation to the impersonal, supportive experience of acceptance?

For many people, acceptance begins with tolerance, a kind of mental and emotional force to counteract the tendency to reject what is happening. When you are aware that you are rejecting a situation or feeling, you can put the brakes on that compulsion and find yourself *tolerating* the situation or feeling, while still not liking it and wanting to reject it. This tolerance will lead to *endurance*, a willingness to remain nonreactive toward the discomfort. This usually involves a certain amount of conscious calm breathing. Instead of gluing your attention to the situation or emotional reaction, you bring your attention to watching your breath go in and out, up and down. Endurance will then morph into *relaxation*. You will notice that when you are not accepting someone or something exactly as it is, there is tension inside you. Breathing may be constricted, and there will likely be tightness in your shoulders, jaws, and solar plexus. Relaxing will bring about a release of tension, thus allowing you to calmly regard the uncomfortable feelings that are at the root of your rejection and *accept* them exactly as they are. It may be helpful to ask yourself the following question from time to time:

"Am I seeing my partner through the eyes of rejection or acceptance?"

Although it seems that many people do start out by first tolerating and going on from there to endurance, relaxation, and ultimately to true acceptance, it does not necessarily have to happen that way. It is possible, when faced with an undesirable event, to simply accept.

> *Yeah, but it could also be impossible to accept! I mean,*
> *don't you have some fear or some pain that, when you're*

feeling it, your body just can't relax, and you're just overwhelmed?

Yes, and at those times, acceptance does seem impossible.

So what do you do at those times?

As best I can, I accept that I don't seem to be able to accept what I'm going through. As best I can, I accept my belief in my humanness. Somehow, that seems to help me be aware of what is beyond *me*.

Moving on now, awareness is an amazingly simple experience, made very difficult and complicated by a person's attempt to make it happen. The difference between being aware and *trying* to be aware is the same as the difference between skiing and *trying* to ski. So much complex mental dialogue is involved when one tries to do something. So many doubts arise, not to mention the pressure to remember the sequence and coordination of steps required, that one spends a lot of time skidding down the slope on one's ass or tumbling down in explosions of snow and ski paraphernalia.

Awareness Exercise

A more direct approach to awareness involves simply noticing. Follow these steps, line by line, doing as each line suggests before reading the next one.

Look at the palm of your right hand for about fifteen seconds.

Simple, right? Now, look at your entire right hand for a while without moving your eyes, but also without focusing on a single point on your hand. Your eyes will probably settle on a specific spot, but this will not limit you from noticing your entire hand.

With your hand held out as it was in the previous step, close your eyes for about twenty seconds and be aware of the presence of your hand.

Next, close your eyes again, this time being aware of your entire body.

Did you notice that awareness is not dependent on your sense of sight?

Now, keeping your eyes open, but without moving them, be aware of the room you are in, including what is behind, below, and above you, including the area outside of the room or space you are in. If you are outdoors, simply be aware of your entire surroundings.

Did you notice that all of your surroundings, along with your body, are all within your awareness? Did you also notice that your awareness is not limited to your senses, as you could be aware of things you could not see, touch, hear, taste, or smell? And did you also notice that your body and the space you were in were not aware of you? Everything you are aware of does not seem to be aware of you.

Now close your eyes again and be aware of that vast, seemingly infinite space inside you—your *inner space.* Notice that it has no boundaries or edges.

How could such a vast inner space exist inside that obviously limited body?

Lastly, close your eyes, and just watch whatever thoughts come to you. Let them pass by as if they were clouds floating by in the sky. Do this for up to one minute.

Did you notice that your thoughts are inside your awareness? Did you also notice that your thoughts are inside your mind, but your mind is also inside your awareness?

Now for the big question.

Did you notice that the ideas of *my awareness* or *your awareness* are inside the awareness? If you are inside the awareness, the awareness can't belong to the person you think of as you, but there is a *you* experiencing awareness. What is that *you* are aware of?

It's not your body, your thoughts, or the person you think of as you. Let's say that the awareness is the ineffable *You* that I have previously referred to, and before I bring this topic back to the issue of relationships, stop to consider the implications of what I just wrote:

What if that awareness is the ineffable *You*?

Wouldn't that mean that all the spiritual seeking people do, all the disciplines and strivings and almost fanatical devotion to the search for truth, are not necessary if the ineffable is that easily accessed? Doesn't the actual search for Truth make the Truth seem far away and disconnected from you?

Now back to the topic of relationships, since that's what this book is about. When you are feeling uncomfortable with your partner, and you are reacting to that discomfort by getting upset, awareness seems to have shrunk itself down and split itself in two parts. There is first the vague awareness inside you that you are unhappy; there is also the awareness that you are unhappy *because of* your partner's words or behavior, as well as the vague sense of the outer world registering your partner's behavior. The outer awareness may be big enough to include your surroundings and the presence of others in the vicinity, but usually most of what little awareness you seem to have is surrounding your partner. At these times, awareness seems very small and limited, making the ongoing conflict seem absolutely huge. Similarly, in your inner space, your hurt, anger, and Persecutor/Victim thoughts seem to take up the entire space of your awareness. This is what I call a *personal experience*, where everything is concerned with what seems to be happening to, and within, your body. Awareness seems to be totally attached to your senses, thoughts, and feelings.

Now imagine that you are sitting in an audience watching a play about a couple embroiled in a conflict—but also imagine that you *wrote* the play and so you know everything that is about to happen. You follow it moment by moment, enjoying how each actor delivers their lines and noticing the set design and lighting, generally taking the whole play in, while also experiencing the feelings that the actors are conveying so beautifully and realistically. In this case, your awareness seems to be much bigger and inclusive, with your inner and outer awareness actually being one awareness. Now although this may still sound like a personal experience, you, as the play's creator, are not in a state of emotional reaction, but are maintaining a greater awareness of an event described in the previous paragraph. With that greater awareness comes a sense of detachment. The awareness is not *your* awareness and is not confined to what the characters in the conflict think of as important.

Imagine that you are an astronaut circling the planet while you listen to a play about an interpersonal conflict. You are aware that this conflict is taking place on the planet down below, but it is one microscopic part of an enormous planet that itself is a microscopic particle in a seemingly infinite universe. The conflict being expressed in the play might assume a sub-atomic importance in the context of your overall experience. Compare that to the initial scene where you are so emotionally involved in the conflict that it becomes the biggest, single most important issue in your life at the moment. The only difference in the three examples—your personal conflict, the play, and the astronaut's perception—concerns the personal boundaries that try to surround the awareness.

Awareness has a secondary quality of being able to reveal what lies beyond the veil of illusion. If the term *veil of illusion* does not resonate with you, you could say awareness reveals what is behind or beyond what appears to you to be real. When you first experience feeling sad, you probably think that sadness is what you are actually feeling. Bringing your awareness into your inner space and embracing the sadness with it detaches you from it on a personal level and allows you to see the impersonal nature of energy—an energy that existed before you gave it a name and judged it as a bad feeling. Deepening, or expanding, your awareness allows you to penetrate the appearance of the vibration and recognize a power that is within the energy, but not vibrating. This power seems to be pure and still, emanating a joyful, peaceful, and loving state of being. All of this, remember, is within the awareness, so if you keep going with the process, even that beautiful power disappears, and down the rabbit hole you go. And what happens in awareness then is ... nothing!

So although there does not seem to be a beginning or end to awareness, your experience of conscious awareness can begin by simply noticing. (I recommend the book *Simply Notice* by Peter Dziuban if you would like a deeper exploration into this topic.) When a conflict arises between you and your partner, take a moment to face what you are experiencing in your inner space. Disengage your attention from the *story* and pay attention to the disquiet inside you. Without analyzing, rationalizing, or justifying what you are feeling, calmly and quietly observe the most prominent feeling, or the jumble of feelings and emotions. Often awareness will naturally move into what seems to be the center of what you are experiencing and process continues to whatever point it is designed to go—peacefully feeling and accepting your vulnerability, enjoying your essence, or falling down the rabbit hole/into the quantum field.

What about the conflict? How does that get resolved?

Oh, that! Well, often it seems to work itself out when the interference of personal reactions is removed. Or you may get an intuitive insight as to how to respond to it. Other times it just ceases to be a problem, even though all the ingredients of the conflict are still there. All in all, the problem assumes the importance it always had, which is very little to none at all.

Lastly, we come to the theme of appreciation and how it manifests and grows once the caterpillar has entered the cocoon. When you consider the expression Awe + Love + Gratitude and consider the meaning of each of those words, the word *appreciation* just doesn't seem to do the experience justice, especially when you look at how it is used in day-to-day life. Consider the following example.

> Bob: Thanks for helping me move to my new
> apartment, Mike. I really *am filled with awe and
> love and gratitude* for it.
> Mike: Uh . . . yeah, right. No problem, Bob. I
> mean, I only lifted a few boxes.

Seriously though, there are moments, once you've entered the cocoon (and sometimes even before that), when you have a direct experience of life and existence that fills you with a jaw-dropping sense of wonder. Your heart expands with love and you want to say a tearful thank-you—though there is no one to say it to and even if there were, no words could do it justice. That kind of appreciation is as good as it gets.

I can see that happening if you're experiencing some-thing wonderful, or at least pleasant, but I just can't imag-ine feeling awe, love, and gratitude when something lousy is happening.

I know, the mind bucks at the thought of feeling appreciation when confronted with a particularly unpleasant or painful situation. However, the situation is neither good nor bad. It's only *lousy* because of your judgment, and we know what that means, right?

Um . . . wait a minute. I knew the answer a minute ago.

It means that you're feeling un—

—comfortable! It means I'm feeling uncomfortable!

Right, and also that a belief is blocking you from seeing the truth at the moment. You can initiate appreciation even in those moments. It starts with recognizing that you are believing something that you know is not really true and acknowledging the existence of that which is beyond belief.

> *I can understand that if my partner is doing something, and I am getting pissed off by it, I could relax into process and eventually get to a point where I could appreciate my partner again. But how could I possibly jump straight to appreciation when I am just pissed off? How could I see anything good to appreciate in that situation?*

It's not about looking for something good in what you see as a bad situation. Bad and good are judgments of situations, and they will come and go. It's a fact of life in this dualistic universe. There will be ups and downs, ins and outs, pain and pleasure—as long as you are living in dualism, or what some people call *living in separation*. But there is a constant *presence* in the experiences of both pain and pleasure, a presence that you can become aware of because it's not hiding—a presence that *can* be experienced.

> *But I thought you said the presence was a loving, joyful, peaceful power. Well, that's good, isn't it? I can't see anything joyful or loving when I'm annoyed with, or just plain angry at, my partner.*

I said that your essence has the qualities that we recognize as love, peace, joy, creative power, et cetera. Those qualities in and of themselves are beyond the *good* feelings that we call love, peace, or joy, but presence is completely beyond feeling. It's sort of like a lightbulb that's lit up, a toaster that's making toast, a watch, and an iPod. One gives off light; the second, heat; the third keeps track of time; and the fourth plays music. What do they all have in common?

They're all human inventions?

Okay, but they all run on something that was not invented—electricity! So even though they are functioning in four different ways, the common denominator is the electricity, without which nothing would work. Presence is like that electricity—it's behind absolutely everything that happens in this world. There are countless manifestations of its power, but *presence* is unbound by any of them. If you could *see* the presence, you would be less attached and, therefore, less affected by your partner's words or behaviors. Appreciation can help you cut through a lot of your rejection of and judgment of your partner. It begins with *recognition*—not recognition with your eyes, but with your heart; not understanding with your mind, but through your intuition.

Recognition is like a bridge across belief. You witness a situation that you don't like, and you say to yourself, "Wow! I really want to judge this situation as wrong, but I know it's not what it seems." Or, "Wow! What's happening seems so real, but I know it's just an appearance." Or there may be times when you say, "I appreciate how real this pain seems to be, but it's really the *presence* in disguise!" (Or the Tao, or what have you, in disguise.) Here are some more examples of how initiating appreciation might work:

> "I really appreciate how much my partner is irritating me, supporting me to relax into process."

> "I really appreciate this money problem, supporting me to see that fear isn't real."
>
> "I appreciate my partner for criticizing me, helping me face my beliefs about myself that are really not the truth."
>
> "I appreciate how perfectly my partner seems to ignore me, supporting me to face my dependency and feelings of unimportance."
>
> "Even though my partner is really angry at me, I appreciate how perfectly my partner is adhering to the script. It's a completely convincing performance!" (Remembering that the creator of the script is *You* will enhance the appreciation even more.)

At first, expressing appreciation may seem artificial, and it will remain so if you do not see the truth of it in your heart. But if you intuitively feel its authenticity, saying the words of appreciation to yourself will help you cut through your emotional reactions and either guide you toward process or attune your awareness to presence immediately.

Acceptance, awareness, and appreciation grow naturally as an individual grows in consciousness. Historically, these qualities were deemed the goals of one's spiritual practice, and to this day, thousands of people practice nurturing these qualities, not knowing that the practice itself often supports the exact opposite of acceptance, awareness, and appreciation.

So are you saying that people who meditate are not growing in awareness and that people who practice forgiveness are not growing in acceptance or appreciation?

Basically, yes. But that does not apply to every single human being. When you are experiencing those three qualities in consciousness, you are in a state of meditation, and there is nothing to forgive. Nor is there any need to *practice* anything since practice is generally an expression of the search for—or the attempt to earn one's right to—the Truth.

But you were just saying that I could practice appreciation even when I'm not feeling it, and now you're saying that practice really doesn't get people anywhere.

I'm saying that, for the majority of people, generally those in the caterpillar stage of life, practice is another one of those trains that goes around in circles. But when you get off the train and begin to move toward emotional adulthood, acceptance, awareness, and appreciation grow effortlessly even though people still feel the urge to apply themselves to reach deeper levels of consciousness. This is why I suggested you could practice appreciation even when you're not feeling it. Some people feel the need to do that for a while, but not usually for very long.

Chapter Appendix

The Polarities

It's important to note that almost nobody is one polarity all the time. Also, some of the descriptions given are not necessarily as extreme for a given individual as they may appear to the reader.

General Traits of the Positive

Big picture: Usually lacking in detail. Positives love to have big ideas but don't want to get bogged down in the minutiae of the day-to-day making of the picture.

Deny and suppress discomfort: Positives seem to believe that emotional pain would kill them.

Sunny attitude: A constant appearance of happiness and contentment, no matter what's going on behind the mask.

Overly trusting: The world Positives want to live in has no bad people, so anyone who comes into their sphere *must be* a good person.

Impulsive decision makers: Because research is too tiresome for them, Positives like to do the first exciting thing that springs to mind or buy the first item that looks good enough and blindly hope the details will take care of themselves.

Want solutions: Problems are too uncomfortable, blame is too unattractive, and figuring out why something happened is too bothersome and time-consuming for Positives. Let's get this thing fixed and move on.

Problem hiders: If they can't fix the problem right away, they deny its existence. If they're not feeling well physically, they are not likely to go to a doctor because the doctor might find something wrong.

"Presidents": Their big ideas and enthusiasm for making things happen bring Positives—more often than Negatives—to the position of president or CEO.

Easy to please: Positives want everything to be nice or uplifting and so will generate a sense of pleasure in most situations they find themselves in. If a Positive went to hell, they would express, "How nice and warm it is down here!" and pull their chair closer to the fire.

Optimists: Thinking that something great will come out of any situation is a lot more pleasant than worrying about the bad things that might happen. A Positive can fall out of a fortieth-floor window and after falling thirty-nine floors will still be saying, "So far, so good!"

General Traits of the Negative

Detail-oriented: Negatives can be obsessive about every little detail of a plan or venture. Leaving no stone unturned makes it less likely that unforeseen mistakes or accidents will arise. Accounting is a good example of a Negative profession because the smallest details are of supreme importance.

Obsess about discomfort: If a Negative checks into a hotel room where there is the faintest trace of a scent of a previous guest's perfume that the Negative doesn't like, they will ask the hotel staff for another, fresher-smelling room.

Cloudy attitude: Negatives have a natural ability to find fault in any situation and so are usually the ones to rain on a parade by indicating all that is wrong in a situation.

Overly suspicious: Negatives are always on guard for how they might be cheated, deceived, or disappointed and tend to approach new acquaintances cautiously. Along with detail orientation, this suspiciousness will put their partners under a constant microscopic scrutiny, looking for the smallest change in behavior or mannerism that would indicate a problem in the relationship.

Research before deciding: What turns Negatives into temporary Positives is a thoroughly researched deal or acquisition. A Negative will spend days tediously researching a product until they are sure they are getting the best bang for their buck.

Want explanations: Negatives are convinced that, if they know why something happened, they can control the situation and, if it's an unpleasant one, make sure it never happens again. Unfortunately, whys often lead to more whys, but the Negative is convinced there is an answer to all whys if one looks hard enough and digs deep enough.

Problem identifiers: Negatives are the ones that always announce the existence of a problem within the relationship through complaints, criticisms, and other such expressions of discontent. The problem is compounded by the fact that Negatives feel guilty about being the bearer of bad news and are already building their defenses before the unassuming positive partner even enters the house.

"Vice Presidents": Because they examine the details of a plan closely and can pick out the inconsistencies or possible unpleasant repercussions, Negatives make a great counterbalance to the positive president.

Difficult to please: Negatives are very particular about what they like and don't like. If their partner hopes to picks out a blue scarf for them as a gift, it had better be the exact shade of blue, the correct material (you know how polyester makes me itch!), and offered at the right time, when the Negative partner is in a receptive mood. Otherwise, the gift giver will be headed back to the store to get a refund or an exchange.

Pessimists (often "realists"): Positives will often accuse Negative partners of being too pessimistic, when the Negatives are simply pointing out what they see are very realistic problems with their partner's plans or dreams. Example:

> P: Let's go to Malaysia for two weeks!
> N: No, it'll be too rainy.
> P: Oh, don't be such a pessimist!
> N: But it's the rainy season there.
> P: Why do you always have to put a damper on
> my suggestions?

This example brings up another point, which is that a Negative partner is one of the few people that can turn a Positive *into* a Negative. This can cause a (positive) sense of satisfaction for the Negative partner and the polarities undergo a sudden reversal.

Negatives act the way they do in order to clear out any and all obstacles to happiness, and they resent Positives for ignoring reality. Positives behave their way because they want to believe that they are already happy; therefore, no obstacles exist—Negatives, the Positives believe, manufacture problems for their own twisted reasons and should just cheer up!

CHAPTER 7

Freedom from Fusion

Principle #7: My partner and I each have our own boat.

WHEN IT COMES TO DEALING with conflict, you find different responses according to your individual stage of emotional maturity. If you examine the model of relationship stages below, you might see a kind of evolution happen in your own partnership. See if you can identify your general location and tendencies when conflict arises in your important relationships.

First Stage (Caterpillar Behavior)

- No attempts to engage in honest communication when conflict arises because you are more invested in protecting yourself and controlling your partner.

- If there is any engagement, it is defensive, through attack or passive aggression (accusations, criticisms, biting sarcasm, etc.), usually followed by withdrawal.

Second Stage (Caterpillar Moving Toward Cocoon)

- Limited attempts to engage, usually defensively, or semi-openly with readiness to run back behind the shield. Continued efforts to control your partner. Some attempts to self-soothe and occasionally to relax into a personal version of process, typically designed to heal or change yourself into a better person.

- Withdrawing from interaction, sometimes to protect yourself and go over the story and other times to face your feelings.

Third Stage (Entering Cocoon, Dissolving Caterpillar Body, Growing Wings)

- Open engagement, sometimes beginning with residual defensiveness, leading to acknowledging your vulnerability without laying blame on your partner as the cause of your pain. When discomfort builds to a point where it seems overwhelming, you will call a *time-out* for process. You may leave the room, but not as a withdrawal or disengagement from your partner—rather, you give yourself some quiet time to disengage from your story and relax into process.

- Little or no attempt to control your partner. Open engagement and continued connection with your partner while relaxing into process.

As we grow toward emotional adulthood, the desire to control our partner diminishes. Typically, control is supported by traditional relationships in most cultures because of what one might call a "one-boat policy." For many of us, the view of marriage has been two people sharing one boat that sails off into the romantic sunset. Usually, it was the man's boat, with the woman leaving behind her family and friends to become a part of his life. Taking on the man's last name and working to support him in fulfilling his dreams and goals, the woman would leave her boat and board the man's, accepting his captaincy. In many cultures, the woman rarely rose above the rank of seaman first class, until her husband died and her son brought her along on his boat. Then the daughter-in-law was the lowly seaman, and mother was promoted to first mate.

I remember once looking through the 1969 high school yearbook of my older brother, Ken. He was only three years my senior, but when it came to the question "What do you want to do with your life?" the difference in the girls' answers was noticeable between his graduating class and my 1972 class. In Ken's class, most of the girls were choosing between "wife and mother" and secretary or stewardess; there was the occasional teacher or nurse or the rare psychologist. It was an unwritten assumption that their professions would last until the girl found the right guy to take her away from all that.

In my 1972 graduating class, the girls' responses indicated a much wider range of choices, including biochemist, engineer, architect, doctor, and other such professions; there were next to no females expressing a lifelong goal to be that of wife and/or mother! There were even some girls who were brazenly claiming that, if they were to get married, they would keep their own last name.

Over the next few decades, I witnessed this attitude growing, with more women attaining postgraduate university degrees, keeping their last names after marriage, going back into the workforce after they had brought a child or two into the world, and, perhaps even more significant, claiming the freedom to get a divorce—even if the husband didn't want her to!

Yet, with all of these marvelous changes, there was still a commonly held belief that marriage was about two people sharing one boat. With the freedom that women were now enjoying, this made steering the boat a very difficult task, as often one partner might desire to sail in a different direction. In those cases, couples were encouraged to work toward complete agreement, but if this could not be reached, a healthy compromise would do. The problem with either of these possibilities was that (a) it could take a very long time to reach a win-win agreement, and often such an agreement never came about; and (b) the only satisfaction that compromise could give a person was in knowing that the other side lost as much as they did. The first case may explain the increase in divorce rates, while the second possibility has been the source material for countless stand-up comedians, who joke typically about what they have to put up with in their partner.

In my experience, complete agreement does make for smooth sailing, while compromise or holding a position in disagreement often has the boat not going where either truly want or, worse, not going anywhere at all. As both husband and counselor, I have come to truly appreciate the issue of agreement in all relationships, not only because of how smooth and peaceful agreement feels, but also because of how much I have learned and grown through the disagreements. I am not suggesting that agreement is essential to relationship, but rather that how you deal with disagreement determines the direction of pretty much your entire life.

Inherent in the word "agreement" is the dependency on two or more parties to reach a decision as to how to function *together*. Without all sides reaching that same decision, there is a belief that relationships will fall apart in a very unhealthy way. Agreement = Healthy Relationship; Disagreement = Unharmonious Association. Ergo, you cannot be in a harmonious relationship unless you are in agreement on all things that affect the relationship. The least desirable, but still acceptable, form is an agreement to disagree.

But how is it that disagreement in a relationship is so often seen to be an unpleasant event? If you disagree in your relationship, what makes it necessary for you to convince your partner to come over to your side? Let's explore these questions further by first considering the critical areas of disagreement in most intimate relationships:

- Sex (frequency, style preferences, attraction to others, mutual satisfaction . . .)

- Money (spending styles, where to invest, spending priorities, whose money it is . . .)

- Children (discipline styles, education, diet, quality/quantity of time spent with them . . .)

- In-laws (influence/interference of parent-in-law, division of attention between in-law and spouse, necessity of adhering to in-laws' values . . .)

- Specialness (amount of attention being paid to each partner; amount of attention *not* being paid to each partner due to work, friends, other interests, hobbies, or addictions . . .)

- Living habits (messiness/neatness, chore distribution, state of health and physical appearance . . .)

The first five areas are generally the most critical in a relationship when it comes to reaching and maintaining agreements, with the sixth sometimes becoming an extremely distracting source of irritation. Eventually, a crisis will emerge in one of these areas where there cannot seem to be any agreement, including the agreement to disagree.

- Partner A wants sex every day, while B is not interested in lovemaking at all. So A turns to porn or decides to have an affair, which Partner B cannot tolerate.

- Money problems reach critical mass when Partner A, who stays home to care for the children, keeps spending money, while Partner B has to work extra-long hours to keep their heads above the water. Then, Partner A discovers the real reason for their debt is that B had been secretly making high-risk investments that all failed.

- Partner A is a firm believer in strictly disciplining the child, including physical punishment "when necessary," but Partner B is absolutely against corporal punishment and has a generally laissez-faire attitude toward raising children.

- Partner A's mother moves in after her husband dies and starts taking over the house, telling Partner B how to cook and clean and demanding that her every request be obeyed. When Partner B complains to Partner A, Partner A takes the mother's side and expects B to be more filial.

- Partner A is spending too much time at work, neglecting Partner B for days. When Partner B complains, Partner A insists it's all for the good of the family, but when Partner A is not working, he/she is meeting friends at the bar or spending hours on the computer at home, leaving B to feel abandoned, unloved, and unimportant.

All these examples were picked from my memory of complaints that arose repeatedly in my counseling sessions or workshops, where couples were trapped in a gridlock of uncompromising disagreement. Both were miserable around each other, and even though one would attempt to dissociate and run up into one of the positive quadrants, ultimately the positivity would wear off and both would find themselves unhappily wishing the other would leave their position on the issue. Often, in these situations, the outcome is either divorce, separation, or what I call the marriage divorce, in which the couple remain under the legal title of marriage, but maintain an aggressive distance from each other. One or both might fall into the discouragement-based behavior of resignation, remaining silently miserable, or dissociate from each other to the point of being (polite or impolite) married strangers.

Once again, I remind the reader that couples in a relationship can only behave according to the state of their emotional maturity and that both individuals in an intimate relationship are typically at the same level of maturity. There is nothing wrong with any level, and you do not grow by thinking that you *should*. Growth occurs as one awakens from one's present state and expands in acceptance, awareness, and appreciation. In the following experiment, it's awareness that seems to be the factor that is required first.

Pop Quiz

Read the following lines and determine where you have found yourself, in the past or present, when it comes to dealing with disagreement:

- Retreat, dig in, and defend your position, even being willing to sacrifice the relationship in order to get your way.

- Retreat, defend your position, and offer your partner certain concessions if they will give you what you want.

- Retreat, defend your position, and seek outside support to reinforce the righteousness of your position. Bring that support to bear in your negotiations with your partner.

- Retreat, and after a while, confront your motivations for stubbornly holding on to a position. Admit that you overreacted and begin to negotiate an agreement, usually only reaching a compromise of some sort.

- Seek to appease the other party, even if it means compromising on some issues that you see as important to you.

- Try to get along at all costs, giving in to the other party's desires, regardless of your own.

- Communicate tirelessly until you reach a completely satisfying win-win agreement.

Before I came upon the idea of intimate relationship involving each partner in their own boat, I was a firm, almost fanatical, adherent to the belief that all conflicts must be resolved by agreement that fully satisfies both parties. Coming to a win-win result involved letting go of positions on both sides of the disagreement. I also believed that, if I gave up my position and started moving toward the center, I would see my wife taking those same steps. Often I would leave my position, but I would not see my wife doing the same from her side, so I would run back to my foxhole and wait for her to make the first move. Since we could not even agree on how the other should drive the car or which route to take for a trip to the supermarket, there were ample opportunities to practice coming to agreement, but very few occasions when we actually reached a full, 100-percent-winning conclusion. Generally, we would reach some form of adequate compromise, but not something truly satisfying—often because I was more invested in being right than I was in reaching true agreement. Thus, my fanatical drive to reach complete agreement often crashed into my wall of defensiveness and insecurity.

Then I noticed that there was one area in which we never suffered conflicts of any significance, and that was with our children. Our approaches to guidance, discipline, health, and education, although not identical, were completely compatible, and the appreciation for each other's parenting attitudes was mutual. Also, we shared an unspoken, almost telepathic bond with each other whenever we had to deal with a difficult issue involving one or both of the kids, and our response was always unified. Whenever one of us reacted out of anger, the behavior could be later discussed and amends quickly made. Parenting was the most harmonious aspect of our marriage, and at first I thought this was because being right was never more important than the well-being of our son and daughter. Later I will illustrate that it was also a matter of our preferences being in agreement, but for now, let's look at the issue of . . .

Being Right

If your need to be right outweighs your desire for agreement, what does being right actually afford you? Happiness? Fulfillment? Peace of mind? In my experience, being right in my most important relationships has never brought me anything but a brief moment of satisfaction, a sense of relief (equally brief), and a strangely guilty feeling that I was right only at the expense of the other person's feelings.

Secondly, if you truly are *right*, why does the rightness need to be defended so vehemently? Surely, the rightness of your position is self-evident. Can't it stand on its own, unprotected?

When I examine these two questions, I come to the conclusion that righteousness is little more than a defense of something that is not *actually true*. Righteousness, you could say, is the armor of belief.

But if I look deeper, I see belief as a kind of defense as well. I ask myself, what could this belief possibly be protecting, and what is it protecting *against*? What feels intuitively true is that belief is often poised to protect the ego *from* the Truth. In my experience, I have often felt the need to defend my beliefs, but I have never, ever, defended or protected the Truth.

Is it possible that all arguments, and almost all disagreements, are simply skirmishes waged on the battlegrounds of the ego? I don't know what ego is or if it even exists, but there is ample evidence pointing to the fact that when people take arguments and disagreements personally, they enhance the miserable experience of separation, and when issues become less personal, there is more harmony and sense of connection between the parties involved.

What Do You Prefer?

Once again, we come to the topic of *preference*. If you are embroiled in a disagreement, where you view the other party as an adversary, you are entrenched in your defensiveness. If you are defensive, you're in discomfort, and that discomfort is your doorway through your defenses to a point of greater harmony and beyond. Once free of your personal defenses, you can become aware of your preferences.

Your preferences reflect your essential nature and what it wants to experience. Your essential nature could be that of an explorer, adventurer, philosopher, teacher, scientist, athlete, artist, meditator, actor, comedian—or any combination thereof—and preference is the desire to express that nature. Your preference may seem like a need, but I experience it more as a pure *desire,* an impulse that originates in my heart (or soul, if I have one). Following that impulse creates an experience of flow in my life, where everything I do or say is easy. Even when faced with apparent obstacles, I don't perceive an adversary or impediment. Instead, an obstacle is simply a signal that it is time to sit and wait and enjoy watching whatever will unfold.

The issue of preferences brings up the possibility for a new paradigm in relationships, one that involves the necessity of each person having their *own* boat. There are times when there is no agreement—times when agreement is impossible—and this is fine. Your preference will take you in one direction, while your partner's preference will take them in another. It does not necessarily mean the end of the relationship, but rather a time for each to have uniquely different experiences. Often partners rendezvous at some point in the future, sometimes even just a few days, or a few hours, later. How long they are apart doesn't matter because they are never actually apart.

> *That sounds like fairy-tale stuff to me. It sounds great, but to think that it could happen in your average relationship seems like pure fantasy.*

I couldn't agree more.

For the *average* relationship, it *is* pure fantasy at this point. For the relationship enjoyed by two emotional adults, it is simply what they experience—two individuals, sharing a loving connection while enjoying their unique gifts and essential qualities. Standing together, but apart, as Kahlil Gibran described in *The Prophet*. Allowing the winds of the universe to blow between them, they remain joined in their hearts, giving each other the greatest gift you could offer your intimate partner: freedom.

> *So what are those of us who are not emotional adults supposed to do in order to reach that freedom?*

Process. Lots and lots of process. And it isn't something you are *supposed* to do; it's just something that's available if and when you remember. Bring awareness to your position in the disagreement and recognize your unhappiness. Accept your unhappy feelings, ignoring any desire to change, fix, suppress, or deny them. Be aware of the unhappiness as a vibration and relax into the center of that vibration. The process will take you wherever it takes you, if you are open to constantly going further, ever further.

I introduced the idea of two boats to bring more awareness to a blind spot in our lives, which is that one boat can easily become a prison, where a couple spends time beating their fists against the walls rather than giving their heads a shake and saying to each other: "Hey, maybe you are not the problem here!"

It's very hard to see this when it seems like you are trapped with the other person, and the only chance of getting away is to saw the boat in half. This leaves both of you separately foundering and desperately trying to build a new boat before you sink and drown.

Okay, say I agree with you, and my partner and I have decided to each have our own boat, after sharing this one boat for a number of years. Where do we find that second boat?

Some people just wake up one morning and find it there. For others, it appears gradually as an expression of their growth into emotional adulthood. It's a different experience for different people, but you will find yourself one day standing alone in your own vessel, waving cheerfully to your partner across a short gap of water. You recognize that your partner is not your source of happiness, and in that one clear realization, the bondage of ownership begins to dissolve. You become less inclined to manipulate your partner into meeting your needs for importance and belonging, and you grow more attentive to, and supportive of, each other's preferences. Without the suffocating, limiting bondage of fusion, you find yourself drawn to the sense of freedom that you want for yourself and for your partner. You truly support your partner as they choose to follow their own preferences, even if it means sailing away without you to wherever that preference takes them—and for however long.

What do you mean by "fusion"?

Fusion is an artificial bond between two people, based on their mutual needs for belonging and importance. At first it feels wonderful to talk about *my* girlfriend (or boyfriend) or *my* fiancé (or fiancée) or *my* wife (or husband). You are both making each other feel special, living in that heavenly space of being *in love*. Specialness feels so good that you want to keep it forever—to have it all for yourself. So you latch on to someone.

"You're mine, all *mine*," you say.

But now that they're yours, they have to follow certain rules, rules about how they have to make you feel special all the time. You will try to control their behavior and speech more intensively, have the final say on where they can go and what they can do.

"Of course you can go out, honey! Go, have fun! Just remember that you are *mine*, and you must follow *my* rules concerning your behavior."

So even when your partner leaves the house, they must behave as if you were standing right beside them, watching everything they do or say.

In a fused relationship, couples tend to impose so many limitations on each other that they are reduced to certain predictable patterns of behavior that remove almost all possibilities for spontaneity, creativity, or surprise within the relationship. Soon resentment, frustration, and the boredom of the *same old same old* sets in, and the more it grows, the less *special* the individuals feel toward each other.

That's a really depressing picture you described.

It is what it is; neither good nor bad. Opportunities come along to dissolve that fusion, but these are often seen as a crisis—a sign that something has gone terribly wrong—but that's because the couple is just not ready or because it is not time for them to accept the opportunity to grow up. In that present state of fusion, no such opportunity even exists in their awareness. But fusion is not a permanent state once you've popped out of your trance and moved into the cocoon. Then freedom becomes more significant than the need to be special.

I don't know . . . It just seems kind of scary to think of giving my partner that kind of freedom. I'll feel like I'm not as necessary anymore. I'll lose my special position in my partner's life. Plus, I'll be alone.

Alone, but not disconnected. After all, isn't it pretty obvious that you, personally, are actually alone? At first, of course, that freedom can be scary, and you may find yourself jumping back into the other boat and trying to cling to your partner once again, but as you trust process more, the thrill of allowing—and sometimes the *pain* of allowing—creates a greater depth of connection to your partner, albeit a less personal one. By supporting your partner and your children and all your important relationships in their need to express their essential gifts and talents, you open yourself more and more to actually *seeing* them as essence. Amazingly, the more you see their essence, the less you need to hold on to them. You find yourself simply being happy that they exist in this phenomenal world. Of course you might miss your partner and your children when you are physically apart, but that will actually enhance your appreciation for them.

Who's Minding the Store?

Okay, I get the idea, although I'm not sure if I can trust that it will all just happen naturally. I mean, I feel like I want to do something or practice something—besides process—to help it along.

Mind your own business.

*What? I'm not . . . I'm sorry, I didn't know I was inter-
fering with your—*

No, I mean you can maybe help it along by *minding your own
business* in your relationship. And let your partner mind his or
hers. Imagine owning a store next to another store, and always
going to that other store to see how they are managing it. This
gives you maybe 50 percent of the time in your day to take care
of your own business—a pretty inefficient way of doing com-
merce. Similarly, in intimate relationships, a person can spend
a great deal of time obsessing about stuff going on with their
mate that is really none of their business.

*But if my partner is upset about something, that is my
business too, isn't it? Especially if the upset is connected to
something I said or did.*

What your partner does and feels is your partner's business. How you feel about, and react to, your partner is your
business. How your partner appears to you is your business
because it reflects what you are experiencing inside, but you
can't reach inside your partner and make a bunch of adjustments in order to make yourself feel better. Let your partner
be, and take care of yourself.

That sounds really selfish.

Quite the opposite, actually. I'm not suggesting that you
don't comfort your partner if they are hurting or in distress. I'm
saying that instead of comforting your partner in order to make
yourself feel better, pay attention to your own guilt, anxiety,

or discomfort while encouraging your partner to do the same. If your partner seems upset and this seems to make you feel guilty, take care of your guilt before—or perhaps while—you respond to your partner's behavior. Your process is your business. Expressing concern for and supporting your partner is your business. What your partner is feeling is your partner's business.

> *What if my partner starts trying to mind my business?*

Again, this bears repeating. What your partner does is your partner's business. How you react to your partner is *your* business. You will either accept or reject, but that is your business and your business only.

> *Aren't there some relationships where, for instance, John wants Mary to mind John's business because then it would prove that Mary cares about John?*

Sure, there are a great number of relationships like that, staggering along in fusion. It's human nature for many people to want their partner to save them, pity them, be jealous of them, give them advice, admire them, what have you. As you grow in maturity, however, the tendency toward fusion dissipates, and differentiation grows.

> *And "differentiation" is . . . ?*

To put it simply, differentiation is the process of sharing a journey in individual boats, giving each other the freedom to follow preferences, and accompanying each other when the preferences are the same.

What if my partner is not into process, or growing, or acceptance, or any of that stuff? I know, I know! It's none of my business, right?

It may be helpful for you to recognize that obsessively thinking about your partner is a way to suffer and avoid pain at the same time.

What? How can I suffer and avoid pain at the same time?

Generally, when you are obsessing about your partner, you are miserable, but so preoccupied with the story and its emotional entanglements that you don't recognize your own unhappiness.

It still sounds really selfish to me to just worry about my own experience and not be concerned about how my partner feels.

There's a big difference between being concerned and being obsessed with how your partner is feeling. Obsession tends to lead to pity, which leads to falling into a Rescuer compulsion. Before you know it, you're struggling through another chapter of the Victim Story. That's not wrong. It will simply become tiresome for you and, ultimately, unnecessary. Exploring relationship as a two-boat experience helps ease the transition from fusion to differentiation—and the freedom of an untethered relationship.

CHAPTER 8

Hear, Hear . . . Listen

Principle #8: Communication with my partner reflects emotional maturity and consciousness.

I USED TO BE an idealistic relationship counselor, believing that perfect relationships were created by two hardworking, sincere, responsible individuals who were dedicated to applying themselves daily to the daunting task of transforming their relationship into a so-called *true partnership*. The task involved healing all their subconscious wounds, being fully accountable for their feelings, being constantly willing to take risks, and practicing honest, effective communication. The day I woke up and realized that every person's relationship was already perfectly designed, the guidelines for *true partnership*, which I had been espousing and struggling to follow myself, revealed the tormenting shoulds at work behind the scenes. One of the main principles that I—and many other counselors—followed concerned communication.

As I stated earlier, the standard of communication for the 300 Percent Relationship required 100 percent honesty, 100 percent accountability, and 100 percent willingness to be wrong. It was a standard that I never lived up to—and one that silently tormented me whenever conflicts arose in any of my important relationships. It required that all my needs for maximum importance and irreplaceable belonging be ignored or somehow caused to disappear because, when you think about it, a great deal of our communication is employed to satisfy the need for *importance and belonging* (and safety and power, as well).

As you get drawn away from constantly attempting to manipulate others, and more drawn to experiencing what *You* truly are, you begin to see communication as a wonderful tool of support for that purpose. To see that more clearly, it may help to understand more about what communication actually is—as well as some of the lingering communication myths that blind us to greater potential.

First of all, communication is not merely an exchange of words. As a matter of fact, words can often be the least important aspect, except, of course, in written correspondence. When you are in the same physical space as your partner, body language claims the greatest importance, followed by paralanguage (tone of voice, pitch, or other vocal effects), and, lastly, words. It is generally believed that the ratio is 58 percent body language, 35 percent paralanguage, and 7 percent verbal use.

I was once in a restaurant in a Chinese city. It was owned by an American man and his Chinese wife. At one point, the man took me aside to show me the patio area and began talking to me about his marriage. When the couple had gotten married, he'd not been able to speak any Mandarin, and she was not capable of too much English. Five years later, they were still not able to talk in each other's language.

At a certain point in the conversation on the patio, he intimated to me that his wife wanted to get a divorce, and he described her reasons for this in great detail. The whole time he was telling me this, I kept thinking, *How the hell do you know she wants a divorce? Maybe she wants a new car or a piece of jewelry! Neither of you knows what the other is saying!*

It was a great example to me of how little actual words are needed in relationship communication. They had both become experts in reading each other's body language and paralanguage. Maybe their paralanguage wasn't even necessary, since, as we all know, body language can speak volumes.

This brings up another point—that partners are *always* communicating with each other. Because of the tendency to polarize, you may find that one person in the relationship is a talker, while the other is a person of very few words. In a fight, one person may be a yeller, while the other withdraws into utter silence—yet the *body language* never shuts up. Ask anyone who has been married for a long time, and they will tell you that they can tell what their partner is feeling by the kind of silence they are expressing. Like a picture, the look on one's face (or the lifting of one finger) can be worth a thousand words.

A third point regarding communication is that most of the exchanges during conflict consist of misunderstandings. This is because we tend to talk and speak through the filter of our defense/control/manipulation/safety mechanism—which is to say our *Defense System*, which I will describe in greater detail shortly.

A fourth point is that communication does not, in and of itself, resolve anything. When you hear someone suggesting that we "talk this thing out," what they are often suggesting is that both parties vent until they are tired of talking and a temporary truce comes about.

Lastly, an important point that is often overlooked is that *listening*, not hearing, is the most important aspect of communication. If you are hearing your partner's message from behind a wall of defensiveness, you will respond from behind that wall. How can any understanding come about from that position? Listening helps you to hear with your heart.

The Circles of Expression

Imagine that the blank space in Figure 8.1 (on the following page) represents the real *You*. It symbolizes that which is beyond time and space; a formless, undefinable power or presence that has no beginning or end. It has been called the Tao; the ineffable; the power and presence of unconditional love; the Universe; and infinite power, intelligence, wisdom, and creativity, among many other names. It is the power that moves everything, but never itself moves. It's the creative force that has never been created, the causeless cause . . . it's *You*, and although the page may be a shade of white, obviously *You* don't possess any color whatsoever. So, take a look at *You*.

Figure 8.1

In *Your* infinite power, wisdom, and love, *You* create an experience simply by imagining it. It's an impossible experience because it exists in dimensions of time and space; whereas *You* have no dimensions and do not exist in time and space. However, because *You* can do anything, *You* create a virtual reality where things can exist in separation, and *You* can experience that separation as if it were real. So *You* begin by creating a quantum field, which is like a bridge between the infinite and the finite. Out of this quantum field, all things emerge.

●

Figure 8.2

Then *You* create *you*, a human being, living in a universe of separate things and beings. *You* somehow put *Yourself* into a hypnotic trance that causes *You* to forget what *You* really are, and so become *you*. *You* are a beautiful *essence*, filled with countless potentials, gifts, and talents, all ready to be expressed through the vehicle of your uniquely designed physical body. Just look at any newborn child, and you will see that pure beauty and seemingly limitless potential shining through.

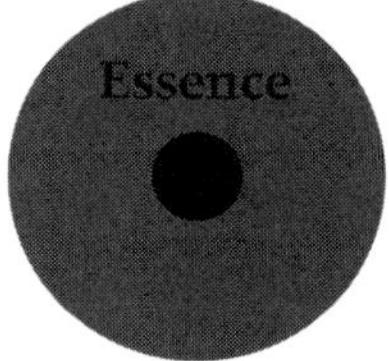

Figure 8.3

In time, the essential you (which is really *You* with amnesia) begins to identify with the vehicle you are in—that tiny, fragile body—and a self-concept gestates. You become more and more aware of the vulnerability and limitations of your body and come to fully believe that this body and mind are who you really are. Some fields of psychology call this ego-body identification. (The word "identification" means the making of an id, or self.) All your beliefs about yourself, other people, life, God, and the world are all extensions of your own self-concept.

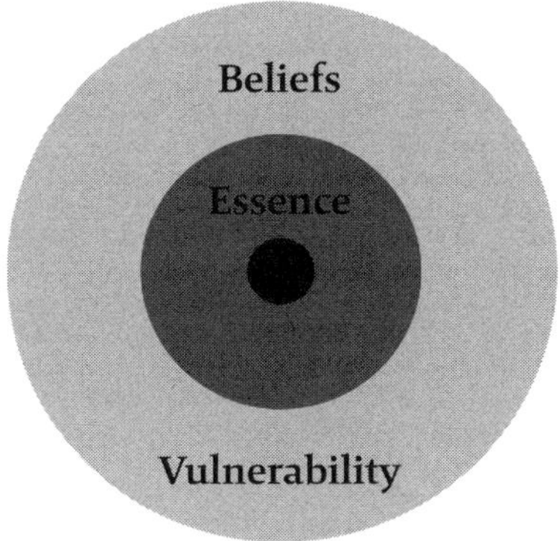

Figure 8.4

Now *You* see *Yourself* as a vulnerable, tiny being in a gigantic world, and you begin to feel all the human feelings associated with that vulnerability and limitation, so another human characteristic begins to grow in you: the need to protect yourself. It is important that your vulnerability is not seen or else—your fear warns—you will be attacked, probably killed! So you must hide your vulnerability, but within that vulnerability are your needs for importance and belonging. Thus, you have to create a system that will (a) protect you from imminent harm; (b) help you get your needs met without revealing the fragility of those needs, if possible; (c) help you also to control your environment to avoid discomfort; and (d) keep you safe and secure from future threat.

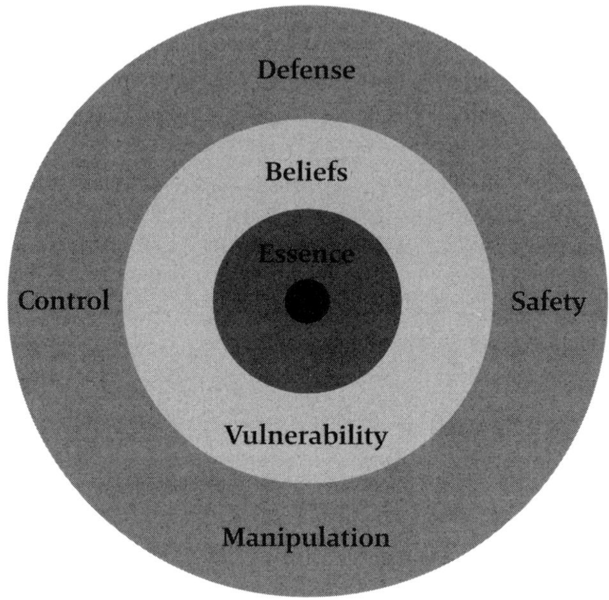

Figure 8.5

To ensure a sense of belonging, most of us create a facade around our defense mechanism; let's call it our *face*. It is a combination of appearance, behaviors, and manners of speech that create a certain image by which we navigate. Some faces are serious, others are cheerful, some are intimidating, while others are seemingly innocuous. Each face is unique in design but identical in intent—to allow the individual to control and manipulate others while hiding their real vulnerability. The outside world rarely sees past your face unless you are severely hurt or expressing some aspect of your essence.

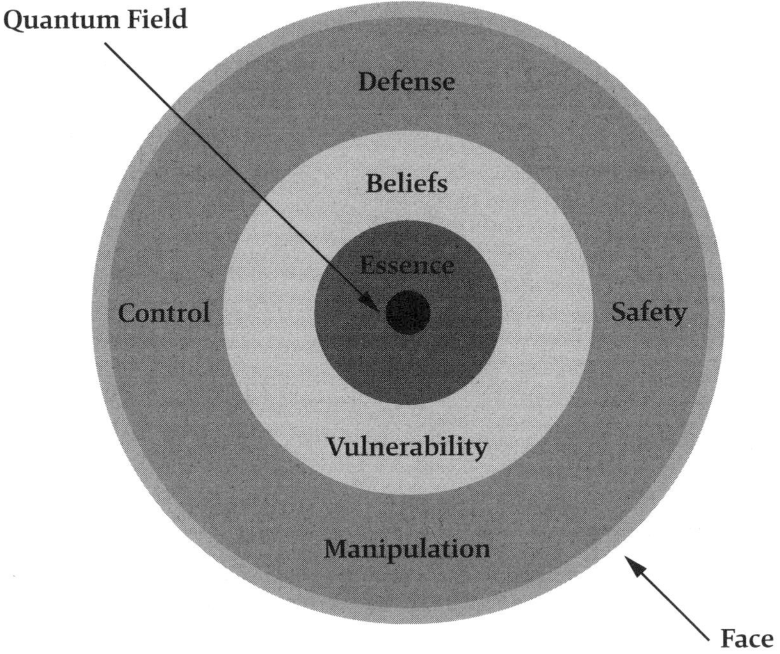

Figure 8.6

And after all the trouble you go to in order to protect yourself from any personal danger, what do you do? You start looking for an intimate relationship! You do the one thing that threatens to penetrate all your defenses and touch you in your most vulnerable places! Remember, it is your *belief* in your vulnerability that blinds you to the truth of what you are. Facing that vulnerability openly will help you dispel those beliefs and allow you to truly *see*. The problem is that you are so entrenched in your defensive behaviors that they have become habitual, compulsively driven patterns that you have come to identify as the *real you.* Any emotionally important relationship will challenge that entire system.

And guess what? Your partner is doing the same thing! Both of you are in a trance of forgetfulness and think *You* are *you,* that physical/mental/emotional identity, with an obsessive need for importance and belonging. So the two of you spend a great deal of time in your relationship (a) protecting yourself from getting hurt, (b) trying to control the other in order to feel comfortable, and (c) manipulating each other into satisfying the need to be special.

Most relationship counseling approaches to communication are designed to help you let go of your defenses and acknowledge your vulnerability so that you and your partner can share your mutual humanness and grow closer in love and acceptance. It can be a beautiful experience of intimacy, and it can help you to touch each other's essence. In my book entitled *Relationship: Bridge to the Soul,* I outlined the communication steps to reaching that point of joining.

Truth-Based Communication

Since writing *Relationship: Bridge to the Soul,* I have come to see that communication can be a wonderful tool for helping me wake up from my trance of forgetfulness and grow in acceptance, awareness, and appreciation of what I really am. Nowadays, my purpose in truth-based communication is *not* to move closer to my wife or help her to better understand me—even though those are by-products—the icing on the cake, so to speak. Instead, such interactions come from the inspiration to let my communication lead me to the Truth.

This type of communication begins with two focal points: (1) noticing *where* you are speaking and listening from, and (2) purposefully altering your vocabulary to reflect consciousness.

Since communication can come from the face, the defense system, vulnerability, essence, or the quantum field and beyond (Figure 8.5), it is relatively simple to stop and notice what you are expressing and whether it is motivated by the compulsive, obsessive, fixated, or addictive nature of personality; the tenderness of your vulnerability; the peaceful beauty of essence; or by the silent power and presence beyond the human. Noticing where you are speaking or listening from can then lead you to a fulfilling response if one is required. You can interrupt the unconscious, compulsive pattern and look beneath your defenses. You can embrace and accept your vulnerability and glide into process. You can enjoy the flow of essence. And you can stare in wonder into the seeming emptiness of the non-self, where only *You* are. It all begins by stopping to notice.

Purposefully adjusting your language to reflect your emotional maturity or consciousness is not necessary, but it seems to be something that many individuals enjoy doing. You may have noticed throughout this book that I have often used the words "seems to be" and "apparently." I initially started using these words when I popped out of my trance because I began to understand that things are rarely what they *appear* to be. Pain was not a bad feeling; it just *appears* that way when we are unconscious. People who you think have hurt you *seem* to be the cause of your discomfort, but they are actually on your side! A coffee table may *seem* to exist, but the more deeply scientists explore the fabric of reality, the more they discover that there's nothing there! There may *seem* to be problems in your life, but the more you face them with acceptance, awareness, and appreciation, the more you get to see that there is nothing to worry about. So I purposely brought these words more into my communications, to support my experiences of acceptance, awareness, and appreciation.

Here are some other examples of this purposeful implementation of words I brought in to support the awakening experience.

When my wife would say something and I would believe that she was irritating me, I would say to myself, "She's an actor in my movie. She *had to* say what she said, because it's in the script!" This would help me to accept her behavior without judgment and focus on my feelings rather than her behavior, and process would ensue.

When a disappointment would occur, I would say (often through gritted teeth at first), "I really appreciate that this happened in order to give me a chance to face and accept my discomfort." At the time I didn't feel the awe, love, and gratitude of appreciation, but I did recognize an opportunity, and that recognition, without rejection, opened the door to appreciation.

When I had a kidney stone attack, I would say, "Shit, this pain seems so convincingly real, but it's actually pure peace and joy in disguise."

> *But how is that different from using positive affirmations or mantras to dissociate from your feelings or deny your discomfort?*

Because I'm wanting to do the opposite of denial and dissociation. I'm drawn to face my vulnerability and accept it exactly as I perceive it so that I can see and experience the Truth of what it really is. Now the phrases I wrote in the examples above may sound unrealistic—nobody talks like that—but when you begin to adjust the language of your thoughts, it is bound to feel awkward and somewhat artificial. To stop and say to yourself, "For me to be reacting like this I must be feeling unworthy or abandoned or heartbroken," can seem unusual, but you might find yourself increasingly wanting to interrupt your behavioral patterns and habits in order to invite greater acceptance, awareness, and appreciation. Apparently it's what many individuals do once they've begun to spin the cocoon of awakening around themselves.

Getting back to truth-based communication, adjusting your vocabulary while talking to your partner may seem even more awkward, but once you recognize the amazing sophistication of your defense/control/safety/manipulation mechanism, you will more clearly see its importance.

The Greatest Adventure Movie Ever Made!

Imagine that you have a priceless diamond in your possession and that you need to keep it safe from robbers. You place it in the center of a room in the middle of a fortress and go about placing defenses, booby traps, minefields, high walls with machine gun–toting guards, and other devices of destruction or diversion. Next, imagine that once the defense fortress is completed, you are standing outside its towering wall, admiring your creation and knowing that you are the only one who possesses the map that could guide you back to your precious diamond. After a few days, you feel a strong desire to go back and look at the beautiful stone. You pull out your map and . . . a gust of wind comes up and rips it out of your hand, carrying it far, far away! Badly shaken, but still determined to see your most prized possession, you try to get back to the diamond. How far do you think you would get? After only a few steps inside, the alarms would sound. You'd be facing bullets, bombs, knockout gas, land mines, barbed wire fences, towering walls, boiling oil, laser beams, and every other form of weaponry known to humanity, from sneezing powder to nuclear missiles! Plus, there would be mazes of mirrors, noises so loud you could not think straight, and dozens of rooms with perfect replicas of your gem in their center, so that, even if you could penetrate all the defenses, you could not be sure you had the right stone.

The above analogy is an example of the sophistication of the defense system *You* created to ensure that it would be virtually impossible for you to remember what *You* really are. It is designed so perfectly that if any country possessed such a sophisticated system it would be unassailable to any adversary. It is often believed that the defense system is created to protect you from your vulnerability, but this is only part of its overall function, which is to blind your awareness to your essence and beyond.

When your partner seems to be doing something that irritates you—either annoys you or makes you feel anxious—the sirens and bells in your defense system go off, without you even being aware that you tripped the alarm. Why? Because *You* designed the system to work unconsciously, *You* set it in place and then threw away the map and all the codes for turning the system off!

Think of a home alarm system. You go on vacation for three weeks, but before you do, you set your alarm system. While you are away, a burglar breaks in and sets off the alarm, causing the police to come around and catch the guy. All this happens while you are sitting on a beach, sipping your piña colada in blissful ignorance. Similarly, when irritated, your internal alarm system goes off, and you turn to passive or aggressive defensive reactions, while *You* are off on some mental beach unwilling to be a part of this uncomfortable conflict. Your communication might be critical, blaming, righteous, wheedling, rationalizing, complaining, raging, or placating, but whatever the reaction, it will be *unconscious*—as you desperately repel any perceived assault on your vulnerability.

An important point: Your entire defense system was built from *unconscious rejection*. Interrupting its patterns opens you to the possibility of *conscious acceptance*.

Stopping to adjust your vocabulary can immediately bring awareness to your inner workings, allowing you to turn off the alarm and begin to dismantle the system. A simple statement such as, "I realize what you've been saying is helping me recognize how unworthy I feel," can stop the power struggle immediately, and invite *process* or appreciation into your circumstance.

> *Sorry, but that sounds unrealistic to me. I just don't see myself fighting with my partner and suddenly saying something like that. I mean, did you do that right away?*

No, not for a long time, as a matter of fact. I started by saying it to myself—and only *after* I withdrew to take a time-out for myself.

I thought withdrawing was a form of power struggle.

Maybe, but I felt I had to take a time-out in order to calm down and look within. Once again, withdrawing, and even power struggle itself, is not *wrong*; it's human. Withdrawing to disengage from the power struggle and invite *process* helps you remember that you are *not* human—rather, you are *You*, having a human *experience*.

Also, when I say I withdraw to disengage from the fight, I am not disengaging from my partner. I'm detaching from the story I was caught up in so I can grow in—

I know, I know . . . so you can grow in appreciation, awareness, and acceptance.

Right! So initially, I did withdraw and gave myself a little talk, adjusting my vocabulary to support that growth. After process, I would return and continue my communication, but I wouldn't return with stronger defenses like I used to. In the past, I would withdraw so as to get my argument more in order, review what I said—and what I *should* have said—and then return more defensive and righteous than when I had left.

As time went on, I could remain engaged in the communication and disengage from my story and my position. I began to adjust my vocabulary while speaking and listening to my wife, feeling the walls melt away as I recognized that everything she said was a support for me to relax and accept.

Does it get any easier?

It gets simpler and flows more, if that's what you mean. Certainly the number of fights in our relationship has dwindled to a brief snit now and then, and the sense of closeness has grown, but neither has been the result of practicing *effective* or even *radical* communication. Your relationships always reflect your stage of emotional maturity, and they are never the cause of emotional maturity. When you're an acorn, your relationship reflects an acorn, and whatever happens is in line with the nature of the acorn. When you become a seedling, the relationship reflects the seedling. Same thing as you grow from there to a seedling, sapling, young tree, and mighty old oak.

> *So if it's a natural progression or maturation, why do I have to practice anything? Why do I have to adjust my vocabulary? You say I don't have any control in my life anyway, and everything happens according to design.*

Do you feel the urge to adjust your mental and vocal vocabulary in your communication with your partner?

> *Well, yeah, if I remember to.*

Can you make yourself remember?

> *No, remembering just seems to . . . I don't know . . . happen!*

Amazing, isn't it? You'll be having this big argument about something really important, such as the proper way to parallel park, or how ripe an avocado should be before eating it, and suddenly, what pops into your head? A reminder to stop, relax, and say something that more clearly points to what is true. And you'll feel an urge to adjust your communication, just the slightest bit, to invite in acceptance, awareness, and appreciation.

> *So, if I remember, I can choose to adjust my vocabu-*
> *lary in order to point me toward the truth, right?*

Well, you could call it a choice to do so, if you like. I am not sure how much choice the personal self has in life, but it often seems that our actions and words come from personal choices, so, sure, call it your choice for now, until you experience otherwise.

To summarize, practicing truth-based communication has no rules to follow—no *shoulds* are there to keep you on track. Whether you are involved in a conflict or not, once you remember to notice from which point you are speaking and listening, you can adjust your vocabulary and communication pattern in order to point yourself toward process, appreciation, or beyond. As strange as it may initially sound to you, you are merely opening paths through your unconscious defenses, so that you can face the vulnerabilities and core beliefs that blind you to what you truly are.

The Truth is right in front of and all around you. You're bumping into it all the time, but your self-concept and beliefs cast a darkness that you have not penetrated. Truth-based communication invites conscious awareness to shine a light into that illusory darkness and show you that what you've been bumping into is what you thought you had to search and strive for. You thought the ineffable was hiding from you, but in fact it was the opposite case.

> *So could we go over the steps, or formula, or whatever*
> *you call them, to truth-based communication?*

The basic principles—not steps or a formula—in truth-based communication are experienced in these questions:

- Am I speaking *and listening* from my defense mechanism, created to protect and deny my vulnerability, and ultimately designed to maintain the trance state of "spiritual" amnesia?

- Is my communication coming from my personal need to be right?

- Am I trying to control my partner in order to avoid discomfort? Am I feeling insecure? Am I trying to manipulate my partner in order to satisfy my need for importance?

- Do I understand my partner's communication? Am I willing to feed back what I heard and how I understood it?

- Can I consciously use vocabulary and speech patterns that are designed to point me toward recognition of the truth (either toward process or toward the spontaneous experience of acceptance, awareness, and appreciation)?

Trust your creativity and your intuition, and what might seem awkward for a short while will support you in having experiences that are wonderfully beautiful and beyond words or imagination.

Can you give me an example of what that might look like in a real-life situation?

Okay, let's go back to the interaction between John and Mary, where John has forgotten to pick up the eggs as Mary requested.

"Did you remember to get the eggs?" Mary asks, as soon as John gets in the door.

"Oops!" John smacks his forehead. "I forgot. Shit!"

Mary rolls her eyes. "John, I asked you to do one thing! How could you forget?"

"No," John smiles, trying to lighten the mood, "you asked me to do *two* things."

"*One* thing! I asked you to go to the market and get eggs."

"See? Go to the market *and* get eggs. Two things. You know I can only remember one thing at a time."

"It's not funny, John. I promised the kids pancakes for tomorrow morning."

"Okay, okay," John says, and becomes aware of the feeling of discouragement creeping into his tone. He reminds himself that Mary is helping him to grow in awareness of who he really is, even if he personally doesn't like the way she is doing it. "I'll go get them now."

"Never mind, dinner's just about ready. I'll have to go out and get them later. You'll probably get the wrong kind anyway."

"I'm sorry, Mary. I guess I'm feeling guilty and defensive toward your reaction."

"Well, how else do you want me to react?" Mary says, raising her voice. "You're always forgetting what I ask you to do. Or else you keep putting it off and telling me you'll do it later." Cutlery clatters as she starts setting the table.

"And you're always finding things for me to do, and then telling me that I did them wrong!" John shoots back, then realizes he's speaking from his defense system.

"Shh! The children will hear you. We agreed not to expose them to our fights."

"I don't want to fight. I'm just feeling really defensive, because I feel that I failed you."

"Well, you sounded angry," Mary says.

"I know. I'm sorry. This feeling kind of took me by surprise and I think I need a little time with it."

Mary stops setting the table and looks at John with sadness in her eyes.

"I didn't realize that I made you so unhappy," she says, her eyes pooling.

"You didn't, Mary. It's just that I was in such a good mood, and then I come home, and suddenly this feeling of failure comes up in me. I wasn't aware of it before we started talking." He places his hand over his stomach.

"Maybe I should leave for a while, and give you time to yourself."

"Honestly, Mary, it's not about you at all. I actually appreciate that you helped me be aware of it—it's a really old and familiar feeling. As far back as I can remember I've always felt that I'm not good enough. I know it's not true, that it's just a belief, but it's a really convincing one."

As John is speaking he pays more attention to the feeling of valuelessness inside, tuning in to the energy of the feeling and letting himself relax more into its center.

"Not that again!" Mary rolls her eyes. John stops doing process and moves back into his defensiveness.

"I was just telling you how I feel, Mary."

"You were just being a wimp, you mean!"

"Hey!" John's defenses now on full alert, he stops himself from blurting out a counterattack and reminds himself once again that Mary is just doing her job, supporting him to face the illusion of his vulnerability. "You're right, I do think I'm a wimp."

Suddenly, John feels very sad, closes his eyes and sinks into the cloud of sadness that seems to be in his chest, thinking to himself, *This feeling is not what it seems; it's really True Happiness in disguise.* He relaxes even more, accepting the feeling exactly as it is, and once more a sense of neutrality permeates his awareness. Neither good nor bad, the feeling is seen as energy, and suddenly he feels a lightness of being. Time seems to slow down and although there are pleasant, joyful feelings in him, awareness has grown beyond feelings. He simply *is.* He opens his eyes and looks at Mary, who now appears to be less upset. He doesn't smile, but does feel closer to her. As the children come into the kitchen, each chooses a parent to approach and hug. He picks his daughter up and says, "Come on, kiddo! If you want pancakes for breakfast tomorrow, you'll have to help me buy some eggs!"

> *That was interesting, but it wasn't very smooth, was it? John went back and forth, and Mary didn't seem to be very different from the way she was in your earlier example.*

Well, I wanted to illustrate that when you are moving toward emotional adulthood, your defense system will still do its job. As you face and go deeper into your vulnerability, the system will try to pull you back to "safety" because it's programmed to see your vulnerability as dangerous. So sometimes when you are trying to do process, the system will attempt to distract you by pulling you back into the story, or bringing in other thoughts, doubts, and criticisms, to name a few of its tactics.

Secondly, I kept Mary's words intact as much as I could to illustrate that your conscious communication doesn't depend on your partner's communication. Even though she was for the most part simply expressing her anger and disappointment, John accepted her behavior as a support for him to face himself.

So, I guess I can expect a lot of that when I try it with my partner—a lot of ups and downs, mistakes and corrections, focus and distraction . . . ?

I don't relate to the word "mistake" when it comes to humans being human. The dynamics of emotional adulthood will do what they do, the defense system will do what it does, vulnerability will be what it is. Everything functions according to design, and the design is perfect. It's not wrong to be angry, quarrel, accuse, or be defensive. It's human. The more you can accept your humanness, the more you will experience the magnificent being that *You* are and have always been.

One more question: Are you *an emotional adult?*

To be honest with you, I have no idea, but I kind of get the intuitive sense that I'm more of an emotional teenager. When I look back, I left home and moved far away from family and friends, but although I had grown up physically, emotionally I was only eight years old, maybe younger. Pain and unhappiness were my enemies, and I would react with anger and fear toward what I perceived as the causes of my misery from the outside world. Most of the time I believed that my unhappiness was caused by my intimate relationships and close friendships, or the lack thereof. As I became somewhat more sympathetic or compassionate toward myself and my vulnerability, I grew a little bit emotionally, but was still very much a child.

At some point, I moved from child to adolescent in the realm of feelings. At that stage, which coincided with my popping out of my trance, I stood between the world of the child and that of the emotional adult. I knew in my heart that my wife and children were not my source of love and happiness. At the same time, I recognized that I still *believed* that they were my source of love and happiness. It was through confronting these beliefs and having a direct experience of the Truth beyond them that I began to taste emotional adulthood. I wrote this book to assist people who have begun to leave, or have left, the emotional-child state, as well as for those who have popped out of the trance of amnesia and are getting acquainted with this amazing realm, where beliefs are exposed as lies that can only exist in the blind state of unconsciousness.

CHAPTER 9

Bonus Material

Author's Note: The ninth principle and the Afterword contain some information and metaphorical explanations about an experience that has been alluded to throughout this book. Even though they may sound abstract, I am using limited words to point to a *direct and immediate experience* of the unlimited. I included this chapter and Afterword as a bonus, for those who are specifically interested in the stage of consciousness that has been called "awakening." I refer to it as the cocoon stage, that time when a caterpillar stops being a caterpillar but is not yet a butterfly.

If you feel satisfied by what you have read up to this point, you need go no further, as the next chapter will not add any new information concerning emotional adulthood. If you would like a little more information about who and what *You* truly are, you are most welcome to read on.

Principle 9: I am the one I've been looking for.

"You know, I just feel that if some seekers I know
were utterly honest, well, they would weep and weep
at the tragedy of all those years of seeking . . . all that
trying . . . reaching . . .
"And they are no closer to what they want even
though they don't know what it is!
"So obvious . . . so simple . . . so vibrantly
apparent . . . just this simple, this edgeless,
unspeakable, scintillating aliveness . . . singing itself
in a wonderment of infinite color and timbre and
hue . . . swirling, pirouetting . . . a dance beyond
compare . . . as there is no other . . . nothing to
compare it to . . . and when the mind stops trying to
grasp what has no edges or handhold, there is utter
relaxation . . ."
—Nancy Neithercut

You are the love and happiness you've been looking for.

When I first heard that statement, I brushed it off as one of the many nice, New Age aphorisms that were coming out at that time. I was still deep in my unconscious trance, so when I read it, I thought the first *you* mentioned was actually me, Christopher. But the truth is I am not Christopher. Christopher is the guy that was constantly looking for that illusive experience of fulfillment: a concoction of love, God, Truth, peace of mind, my perfect mate, enlightenment, and a bunch of other concepts all meant to signify that which would fill me permanently and end my frustrating quest. I was looking for some power out there that could improve, heal, save, and transform the person I thought I was into a perfectly happy Christopher forever.

Have you ever been in a similar position to the one I just described? And did you ever stop to wonder what it is that you are actually looking for in your life? Perhaps your history—like that of many of us—consists of one long pursuit of some*thing* or some*one* that can give you what you have hungered or thirsted for. Considering all your achievements and close relationships, have any of them really and truly satisfied you to the point of not needing anything anymore? It is a mystery that baffled me for decades, wondering what it was that drew me to desire certain specific things like a car, a house, a career, money, a healthy attractive body, recognition, or even fame.

Often, after an achievement or acquisition, I would feel one of two things, either a certain sense of temporary relief and satisfaction or empty disappointment. If it was relief and satisfaction that I felt, I would ride that pleasant wave for a few days, perhaps even a week or two, but eventually I would be hungry again, and my mind would focus on other potential achievements or acquisitions. If I was beset with empty disappointment, I would drop into a depression for a period of time, until I conceived of another achievement or acquisition I could pursue.

My pursuit of intimacy in my teens and early adulthood was much the same. I don't know why I would home in on one particular girl to be my personal savior who would quench my thirst for that perfect love. Often, it would not be a question of appearance—well, not *entirely* a matter of appearance—as much as that of a playful personality, a sense of humor, or a kind of gentleness and understanding.

But what would being with a person like that actually *give me*? Whatever I got from those relationships, it did not last that long before the uplifting titillation of puppy love wore off, and the dissatisfying thirst would take over once again. Being a hopeless romantic, I would fall for one girl after another, sometimes reaching the stage of boyfriend/girlfriend, and other times being turned down in favor of some other guy. Time went on and the girls became women, but my pursuit of that "perfect mate" never aged.

Besides seeking the perfect mate, pursuing achievements and acquisitions, and looking for trustworthy friendships, the undefinable thirst also urged me to a spiritual search for what I thought of as *the Truth*. Having given up on the idea that an anthropomorphic God existed when I was fourteen years old, I became drawn to fundamental questions such as "Who am I, and why am I here?" and "What is my purpose and my life mission?" and "Why is there so much suffering and injustice in the world, and more important, how can I avoid it if possible?"

I thought the truth could be understood through words. I thought there was an actual answer to my questions that could satiate me once and for all, so I looked for the answer in spiritual teachings, philosophy, and psychology. I adopted attitudes of positive thinking, laws of attraction, meditation, vegetarianism. I attended spiritual meetings, and I launched myself on a program of personal growth and spiritual healing. And of course, continued my search for the perfect mate!

The sense that I was so close to the answer—close enough that I could feel my mind reaching out and just about, but not quite, touching it—almost drove me mad with frustration and despair. This was aggravated by a number of relationships that, instead of making me feel loved for who I am, served to make me more and more aware of how unlovable I believed myself to be. Life provided me with many signs and messages along the way, and although I did not recognize or appreciate them at the time, there were some that niggled away at me long after I had seen them. These include:

"The fish in the sea are dying of thirst."
—SAINT KABIR

"Happiness makes you happy."
—MAHARAJI

"Glamour fools you into thinking that there is
some special teacher, path, technique, or teaching
that will lead you to the Truth."
—RON SPENCER

"You can't find what is not hiding."
—ANONYMOUS

"You are the one that you've been looking for."
—ANONYMOUS

Then one day I had a revelatory experience of such intensity that my search immediately ended there and then. As the experience remained and accompanied me throughout my days, I found that everything I thought I needed from my wife and children became less and less relevant or imperative, while at the same time my appreciation (Love + Awe + Gratitude) for them grew.

I could sense the presence of the entity inside me that craved importance and belonging—correctly or not, let's call it "ego." But it seemed like I was no longer looking from inside that ego. Suddenly, it was inside Me. *I* am the one that I was looking for. But I could never find Me any more than a fish in the ocean can find water. I am Me. I am Me, experiencing the phenomenon of being me, Christopher. Christopher's wife, children, and everyone else and every thing are part of that temporary phenomenon, whether it's called an illusion, virtual reality, or a dream. I have no idea what happens to Christopher or any of the other characters once the *dreamer* wakes up from the dream, and that's okay.

A very weak analogy would go something like this:

There *You* are, the infinite being with unlimited creativity, wisdom, love, power, and joy, and *You* decide to do the impossible (which is not a word *You* buy into at all). *You* decide to experience *not* being one infinite, wholly complete being, but instead, an infinite number of separate beings and things! I mean, when *You* want to experience separation, you don't settle for half measures—*You* really go to town with the idea! Just examine the evidence: Here you are, an individual, reading this book, which exists separately from you. The eyes that see the words are a separate part of the body, separate from the brain, which itself has somewhere in the neighborhood of 100 billion neurons—complex cellular structures—which in turn are composed of molecules, atoms, subatomic particles, quarks, strings, or whatever . . . (as you can see, I skipped a lot of science classes—I had to work on my tennis serve). Countless individual pieces go into the one experience of a human being reading a book! And *You* are all of those pieces.

Now in order for *You*, the ineffable being, to have the wonderfully complete experience of being human, you begin in Stage 1 and

- Hypnotize *Yourself* into forgetting what *You* really are and . . .
    - Convince *Yourself* that *You* are *you*, with all your human characteristics, human beliefs, and human limitations; now, you are the opposite of *You*
    - Immerse yourself in an illusionary environment that reinforces your human beliefs and experiences, so that there is no chance of you waking up from your trance and remembering the truth of what *You* really are
    - Spend a great part of your life looking for people and things to give you something to satisfy the never-ending human hunger inside you (look for money to make you feel secure; find work to make you feel capable and useful; seek a position of authority to make you feel powerful; adopt a spiritual or religious philosophy to comfort you and give you an empowering sense of righteousness; pursue friends and family connections to give you a sense of belonging . . . and look for that one true love to make you feel *special*)

- At some point (and no one seems to know when this point shows up) you move onto another stage where you—
    - Wake up and realize, *through direct experience*, that you are not the mental/emotional/physical being

> that you believe yourself to be (this is not a philo-
> sophical, psychological, or emotional event, but
> rather an experience of pure consciousness)

- ∘ Have consistent (but not constant) experiences of the power and presence that exists beyond your beliefs, and beyond the realm that is referred to as "the real world"
- ∘ Watch your beliefs fade or dissolve altogether and experience the True Happiness that had previously been obfuscated by your beliefs
- ∘ Become filled with appreciation for the awesome-ness of life and the amazing design of the human journey; you appreciate how *You* hypnotized your-self into believing you were only human, and how *You* limited your ability to *see* beyond this virtual reality of time, space, and thought
- ∘ Not only understand but directly experience the famous lines from a William Blake poem:

> *To see a world in a grain of sand,*
> *And heaven in a wild flower,*
> *Hold infinity in the palm of your hand,*
> *And eternity in an hour.*

And then there is the next stage.

I have read of the "butterfly stage," where fear falls away, and one is in a constant state of "knowing," but since I cannot claim to have such a constant experience, I won't try to describe it further. It's important to remember that no stage is better than the next, just as no stage in the life of an oak tree, from acorn to mighty old oak, is better than another. Different, not better.

There is no knowing how long an individual will remain in a stage, and there may well be stages beyond the ones I've delineated, but I'm not aware of anyone who *willed* themselves from one stage to the next or interfered in any way with their unique design and script. As a matter of fact, these transitions seem to occur *in spite of* an individual's drive and determination or fear. And all your relationships seem to morph to reflect whatever stage you are in. Sometimes your partner's behavior seems to undergo a drastic change, and it's easy to believe that the change came from your partner, when in fact you are simply *seeing* him/her differently. And all of this happens to you and your partner spontaneously—actually in spite of your best efforts to control your life.

> *So are you saying that I have no control in my relationships—intimate or otherwise? That I'm just a puppet being controlled by invisible strings?*

I don't know. I haven't seen any evidence of control in my relationships. I can't control what my wife, children, or friends will do or say, and I wonder if I can even control what I do or say. All I am aware of is that I seem to be growing emotionally, but I cannot say I've done anything to help or hinder that growth along. So yes, maybe I am a puppet and the ineffable Tao is the puppeteer. And maybe *I* am the Tao as well.

My intuition and my experience tell me that relationship is perfectly designed to help me answer the following three questions:

Who am I?

Why am I here?

What do I do with my life?

If this feels true in your heart, then you would come to realize that the particular body *You* are in can do whatever *You* want it to do. As consciousness grows, what you do shifts *from* the unconscious, compulsive drive to get your needs met, prove your value, and protect yourself and morphs *into* the kind of behavior that reflects a peaceful sense of being. Sometimes you will do just to do, while at other times you will follow an individual preference according to the unique character *You* have chosen to be, but either way, the caterpillar habits will fall away as the heart of the butterfly begins to beat in you.

Now you may think that your partner is a separate being from you, but instead of looking at what separates you, maybe you could consider what is the same. Besides the fact that each organ in your bodies has an identical function, and your minds both generate thoughts in the same way, one of the most obvious areas of being exactly alike is in the realm of feelings. You and your partner have the exact same feelings, both pleasant and unpleasant. As a matter of fact, you might even begin to notice that you and your partner have the exact same feelings at the exact same time! This is easy to see when conflicts arise and you begin to share with each other the underlying experiences. Once you recognize that the same feeling is occurring in two different bodies, you somehow feel *closer* to your partner, even though you have not physically moved closer. That is a taste of emotional adulthood. And that is what I wish for all of us.

And we live happily ever after!

Afterword

I WAS SITTING IN A HOTEL ROOM one day when I had an experience of what I have come to call *waking up*. It seemed that I entered a permanent state of awareness that I cannot adequately describe, while at the same time mysteriously recognizing that nothing really happened and that I had always been in this state. I understand that what I just wrote may sound confusing, so I won't try to describe it any further. Instead I will limit myself to what this experience has to do with this book. This one, ongoing, and direct experience has transformed my marriage and parenthood more profoundly than any amount of work or study of relationship had done for me in the previous thirty years. And the most amazing part is that it came upon me without any effort whatsoever on my part. This *waking up* allowed me to see all my important relationships in a new light, and I understood the amazing design of relationship and its actual purpose.

Therefore, this book is not a guide or manual with suggestions about how to improve or heal any of the important partnerships in your life or make them more exciting and passionate. It's not an instruction manual on how to be a better communicator, lover, friend, or parent. It's about how your relationship is perfectly designed to help you experience pure andlasting happiness. As this happiness fills you more and more, it infuses all the aspects of your relationship.

I am not trying to offer a philosophy about relationship because philosophy is simply an organized collection of beliefs. One of the effects of waking up is a clear recognition that no belief is true. At the moment I woke up, I suddenly experienced belief as a kind of prison, the walls of which blinded me from knowing the truth. When those walls seemed to dissolve, I could see the ineffable Truth that lay beyond all belief, and that revelatory awareness has never left me since that day. I know what *true happiness* is, and when we think we can find that happiness through an achievement, acquisition, or interpersonal exchange, we are simply believing something that is not true.

I use the word "awakening" to denote a process of movement between the unconscious and conscious states of being. At first I hesitated to use any of these terms for this book, as the meanings I assign to consciousness and unconsciousness may conflict with the reader's definition. Finally, I decided to employ the terms and do my best to add comments to remind the reader of the definitions as they apply within this writing.

I often compare awakening to the cocoon (or chrysalis) stage of a caterpillar's/butterfly's life cycle. Just as the form of the caterpillar is dissolved and a new entity—the imago—begins to emerge, the wall and structure of your beliefs begin to crumble and you sense the *presence* (the *You*) beyond belief. There are increasing experiences of the moment beyond time that seem to come and go without any particular pattern. You becomeincreasingly aware that beliefs and limitations have no real power. You keep believing—out of habit, so to speak—but at the same time your beliefs seem more translucent and obviously not the truth. In the awakening stage, you sense, or directly experience, that the world is an illusion, dream, hologram, or virtual reality. You think it's real because you are in some sort of trance, which causes you to forget who *You* really are, and convinces you that you are an ordinary human being whose value is defined by what you can and cannot do or be. You also understand that you are emerging from this trance.

When I first came into this stage, I was overwhelmed by a sense of what I have come to call *presence* permeating everything, including the person I thought of as me. Previously I had experienced a few light drops of consciousness, but they quickly vanished, and the solid wall of beliefs reappeared, leaving me only with a vague sense that something profound had occurred. But upon awakening, I had a more continuous sense of the presence of the *ineffable*, which is greater than words can express. I have become consistently (though not continuously) aware of the egoic impulses, and I no longer see them as adversarial or threatening. I can lose my grip on time and see past and future as broad belief systems. I can observe my thoughts in a more detached way and can watch myself watching myself! This led me to the experience of *process*, which is a key element in this book.

As I stated previously, the experience of waking up from the trance and the ongoing experiences of acceptance, awareness, and appreciation have transformed my marriage and my relationships with all human beings, and so I offer this book to assist others who have just popped out of their trance, and to those who are preparing to do so (even if they don't know it yet). If you've gotten this far in the book, that probably means you!

"When you stop asking life to 'make you happy'—
when you sense, at least occasionally, this inner
stillness—then life is allowed to be itself, as it comes,
moment to moment."
—Jan Fraser

"Ditto."
—Chris G. Moon

Index

About the Author

Chris Moon is a husband, father, life coach, lecturer, and workshop facilitator working in North America and Asia. For over 30 years, he has focused on the direct experience of true happiness and its transformational influence on interpersonal, family, and intimate relationships. His unique approach combines practical information with experiential learning, allowing for the beneficial application of this information to real life situations.

As an author, Chris wanted to approach the fields of relationship and spiritual growth with simplicity and humor because, as he put it, "I always enjoyed the funny teachers in school—they made the driest subjects worth coming to class for. So I thought, maybe serious subjects like family, relationship, and non-duality don't have to be delivered so seriously."

Perhaps because of this approach, Chris' books on intimate relationships, as well as those on consciousness and non-duality, have reached hundreds of thousands of readers in Asia and North America.

Chris loves the great outdoors and enjoys skiing, biking, jogging, and hiking with his wife, Su Mei. Together they founded Vision Mountain Training Inc. They live in the beautiful province of British Columbia, Canada.

For more information on his work,
visit www.visionmountain.com.